TEACHING COMPETENCY OF PRIMARY SCHOOL TEACHERS

TEACHING COMPETENCY OF PRIMARY SCHOOL TEACHERS

Dr. Vinod Kumar Singh

GYAN

The publication of this book was financially supported by ICSSR and the responsibility for the facts stated, opinions expressed or conclusions reached are entirely that of the author and ICSSR accepts no responsibility for them.

The work of this book was evaluated by Professor (Mrs.) Sudesh Mukhopadhyay, NUEPA, New Delhi on behalf of the ICSSR.

Teaching Competency of Primary School Teachers

ISBN: 978-81-212-1039-3

Published in 2010 in India by
Gyan Publishing House,
23 Main, Ansari Road, Darya Ganj,
New Delhi-110002
Phones : 23282060, 23261060
Fax : 011-23285914
E-mail: books@gyanbooks.com
Website: www.gyanbooks.com

Lasser Type Setting by: Quick Media, Delhi
Printed at : **GIAN RIDHI OFFSET PRINTERS**

Dedicated to

Prof. K.P. Pandey

Ex. Vice-Chancellor, M.G. Kashi Vidyapith and
Director
Society for Higher Education and Practical
Applications
(SHEPA)
Nibia, Bachchaon, Varanasi-221011, U.P.

In token of deep regards for his affectionate and
inspiring guidance

Contents

List of Tables 9

List of Figures 13

Abbreviations Used 17

Foreword 19

Preface 21

1. Primary School Teachers and Teaching Competency **25**

1.1 Introduction

1.2 Conceptual Frame work

1.3 Classification of Teacher Competencies

1.4 Emergence of the Problem

1.5 Need and Justification

1.6 Statement of the Problem

1.7 Objectives of the Study

1.8 Hypotheses of the Study

1.9 Operational Definition of the terms used

1.10 Delimitation of the Study

1.11 Organization of the Book

2. Studies Conducted in the Past **57**

3. Design and Procedure of the Study **79**

3.1 Introduction

3.2 Method

3.3 Population

3.4 Sample

3.5 Procedure of Sampling

3.6 Nature and Size of the Sample

3.7 Variables of the Study

3.8 Data Collection Devices

3.9 Development of Teaching Competency Test for Primary School Teachers

3.10 Statistical Analysis

4. Results of the Study on Teaching Competency of Primary School Teachers **97**

4.1 Level of Teaching Competencies

4.2 Gender-Wise Analysis of Teaching Competency

4.3 Academic Qualification-Wise Analysis of Teaching Competency

4.4 Professional Training-Wise Analysis of Teaching Competency

4.5 Habitat-Wise Analysis of Teaching Competency

4.6 Teaching Experience-Wise Analysis of Teaching Competency

4.7 Academic Stream-Wise Analysis of Teaching Competency

5. Teaching Competency of Primary School Teachers **151**

5.1 Conclusions

5.2 Implications of Findings

5.3 Suggestions

Appendix–A Teaching Competency Test 161

Appendix–B Data Collected on Primary School Teachers 183

Bibliography 195

Index 203

List of Tables

1.	1.1	Comprehensive list of Competencies identified as in practice among Primary School Teachers	38
2.	1.2	List of Competencies not-practiced according to Majority of the Primary School Teachers	39
3.	3.1	Total Sample of Teachers	84
4.	4.1	Distribution of teachers at different levels of Teaching Competencies	98
5.	4.2	Gender-Wise Comparison of teachers for their Teaching Competencies	101
6.	4.3	Qualification-Wise Comparison of teachers for their Teaching Competencies (Educational Activities)	103
7.	4.4	Qualification-Wise Comparison of teachers for their Teaching Competencies (Contextual)	106
8.	4.5	Qualification-Wise Comparison of teachers for their Teaching Competencies (Transactional)	108
9.	4.6	Qualification-Wise Comparison of teachers for their Teaching Competencies (Content)	110
10.	4.7	Qualification-Wise Comparison of teachers for their Teaching Competencies (Development of Teaching-Learning Material)	112

11.	4.8	Training-Wise Comparison of teachers for their Teaching Competencies (Educational Activities)	116
12.	4.9	Training-Wise Comparison of teachers for their Teaching Competencies (Contextual)	118
13.	4.10	Training-Wise Comparison of teachers for their Teaching Competencies (Transactional)	120
14.	4.11	Training-Wise Comparison of teachers for their Teaching Competencies (Content)	122
15.	4.12	Training-Wise Comparison of teachers for their Teaching Competencies (Development of Teaching-Learning Material)	124
6.	4.13	Habitat-Wise Comparison of teachers for their Teaching Competencies	128
17.	4.14	Teaching Experience-Wise Comparison of teachers for their Teaching Competencies (Educational Activities)	131
18.	4.15	Teaching Experience-Wise Comparison of teachers for their Teaching Competencies (Contextual)	133
19	4.16	Teaching Experience-Wise Comparison of teachers for their Teaching Competencies (Transactional)	134
20.	4.17	Teaching Experience-Wise Comparison of teachers for their Teaching Competencies (Content)	136
21.	4.18	Teaching Experience-Wise Comparison of teachers for their Teaching Competencies (Development of Teaching-Learning Material)	138

22.	4.19	Academic Stream-Wise Comparison of Teachers for their Teaching Competencies (Educational Activities)	142
23.	4.20	Academic Stream-Wise Comparison of teachers for their Teaching Competencies (Contextual)	144
24.	4.21	Academic Stream-Wise Comparison of teachers for their Teaching Competencies (Transactional)	145
25.	4.22	Academic Stream-Wise Comparison of teachers for their Teaching Competencies (Content)	147
26.	4.23	Academic Stream-Wise Comparison of teachers for their Teaching Competencies (Development of Teaching-Learning Material)	148

List of Figures

1.	4.1	Graphical Presentation of Teaching Competencies of Primary School Teachers	99
2.	4.2	Mean scores on Teaching Competency obtained by Male and Female Teachers	101
3.	4.3	Mean scores on 'Educational Activities' Dimension of Teaching Competency obtained by Teachers having Different Qualifications	104
4.	4.4	Mean scores on 'Contextual' Dimension of Teaching Competency obtained by Teachers having different qualifications	107
5.	4.5	Mean scores on 'Transactional' Dimension of Teaching Competency obtained by Teachers having different Qualifications	109
6.	4.6	Mean scores on 'Content' Dimension of Teaching Competency obtained by Teachers having different Qualifications	111
7.	4.7	Mean scores on 'Development of Teaching-Learning Material' dimension of Teaching Competency obtained by Teachers having different Qualifications	113
8.	4.8	Mean scores on 'Educational Activities' Dimension of Teaching Competency obtained by Different Training Groups of Teachers	117
9.	4.9	Mean scores on 'Contextual' dimension of Teaching Competency obtained by different Training Groups of Teachers	119

10.	4.10	Mean scores on 'Transactional' dimension of Teaching Competency obtained by different Training Groups of Teachers	121
11.	4.11	Mean scores on 'Content' dimension of Teaching Competency obtained by different Training Groups of Teachers	123
12.	4.12	Mean scores on 'Development of Teaching-Learning Material' dimension of Teaching Competency obtained by different Training Groups of Teachers	125
13.	4.13	Mean scores on Teaching Competency obtained by Rural and Urban Primary School Teachers	129
14.	4.14	Mean scores on 'Educational Activities' Dimension of Teaching Competency obtained by different Experience Groups of Teachers	131
15.	4.15	Mean scores on 'Contextual' dimension of Teaching Competency obtained by different Experience Groups of Teachers	133
16.	4.16	Mean scores on 'Transactional' Dimension of Teaching Competency obtained by different Experience Groups of Teachers	135
17.	4.17	Mean scores on 'Content' Dimension of Teaching Competency obtained by different Experience Groups of Teachers	137
18.	4.18	Mean scores on 'Development of Teaching-Learning Material' Dimension of Teaching Competency obtained by different Experience Groups of Teachers	139
19.	4.19	Mean scores on Competency of 'Educational Activities' obtained by Teachers from different Academic Streams	143

20. 4.20 Mean scores on Competency of 'Contextual' obtained by Teachers from different Academic Streams 144

21. 4.21 Mean scores on Competency of 'Transactional' obtained by Teachers from different Academic Streams 146

22. 4.22 Mean scores on Competency of 'Content' obtained by Teachers from different Academic Streams 147

23. 4.23 Mean scores on Competency of 'Development of Teaching-Learning Material' obtained by Teachers from different Academic Streams 149

Abbreviations Used

B.Ed.	Batchelor of Education
BTC	Basic Training Certificate
G	Graduate
H.S.	High School
Inter	Intermediate
JBT	Junior Basic Training
P.G.	Post Graduate
T.C.	Teaching Competency
VBTC	Vishishth Basic Training Certificate

Prof. R. J. Singh
Ex. V.C., M.G. Kashi Vidyapith, Varanasi
&
Ex. Pro-V.C. & Dean, Faculty of Education Lucknow University, Lucknow

Residence
C-385, Sector-6, Indira Nagar Lucknow-226016, U.P.
Phone : 0522-2343555
Mob. 09415159384

Foreword

It gives me great pleasure in writing this foreword to Dr. Vinod Kumar Singh's book : "Teaching Competency of Primary School Teachers". He has worked under me for quite some time during his early career in the Department of Education, Lucknow University, Lucknow. I always found in him a very inquisitive, hardworking, sincere and dedicated person. I am happy to learn that he has cultivated his earlier qualities and abilities further and by now crossed several steps of success.

The book under reference, authored by Dr. Singh, is outcome of his Doctoral thesis in the area of Primary Education. Importance of primary education cannot be overemphasized. It serves as the foundation for future career of children and hence its quality has to be ensured at any cost. The quality of any education system depends upon the quality of its teachers. It is a well-admitted fact that no system of education can rise above the level of its teacher just as a river can never rise above the level of its source. Looked from this angle, Dr. Singh's exploration into teaching competency of primary school teachers as reported in this book is a welcome effort.

The theme of this study is not only interesting but also of great significance for the primary school teachers, primary teacher-educators, educational policy planners and administrators. It is also equally useful for parents in so far as they are the real first teachers, of course informally of their children. Selecting a representative sample and using appropriate research design and statistical techniques, the author has very well analyzed the teaching competency levels of primary school teachers of Lucknow and examined the relationship of different components of teaching competency with variables like gender, academic qualifications, professional training, habitat, teaching experience etc.

I congratulate Dr. Vinod Kumar Singh for his successful efforts in bringing out this first volume. I wish him many more in the years to come.

Date: April 27, 2009
Lucknow

R.J. Singh
Former Vice-Chancellor
M.G. Kashi Vidyapith, Varanasi and
Former Head & Dean of Education
and Pro-Vice Chancellor,
Lucknow University, Lucknow

Preface

Problem of education in India is mainly related to the demand for a growing number of qualified and professionally competent teachers through whom alone can the true objectives of education be realized? Though few educational institutions have a competency based human resource system, most of the public and private sector institutions are still striving to implement it. This book mainly focuses on the teaching competency primary school teachers with respect to different variables. It is supported by a rich research base. It will be useful for primary school teachers, policy makers, administrators and also for those who carry on research as a professional activity.

The present work is the output of author's four year experience of teaching and research. This book is also based on rich and upto date review literature related to teaching competency. The contents of the book have been divided into five chapters.

Chapter I 'Primary School Teachers and Teaching Competency' provides the basic knowledge of teaching competencies. Different classifications and definitions of teaching competencies have also been discussed in this chapter. Emergence, need and statement of the problem have been discussed in detail. Objectives related to academic qualification, gender, habitat, teaching experience, academic stream, training and hypotheses have been covered in this chapter. Towards the end of this chapter delimitations and organization of the book have been discussed.

Chapter II covers, 'Studies conducted in the past'. Sufficient coverage on studies related to teaching competencies of primary school teachers has been given. An honest attempt has been made to include the national and international studies related to different variables e.g. academic qualification, gender, habitat etc.

'Design and Procedure of the Study' has been discussed in chapter III. Here, the details of methodology, sampling, variables etc. have been discussed. Different steps of development of tool have also been discussed in detail in this chapter. Finally the reliability, validity of the tool and scores of data decided through the specific procedures have also been incorporated here.

Chapter IV named as 'Results of the Study on Teaching Competency of Primary School Teachers' covers analysis of data, results and their interpretation. Objective wise analysis covering tables and graphs has been given in detail in this chapter.

Chapter V 'Teaching Competency of Primary School Teachers' elaborates objective wise findings covering different variables undertaken in this study. Implications of findings have also been discussed here in detail. Suggestions for policy makers, teacher educators and future researchers have also been given here.

Attempts have been made to make this text as lucid as possible. Efforts have also been made for maintaining articulation, balance, continuity and consistency in various topics. However, I look forward to seeking comments and suggestions from all educators and particularly primary school teachers, policy makers and researchers for further improvements in the future edition of this book.

First of all I wish to thank Indian Council of Social Science Research, New Delhi for financing this work and Dr. P.P. Pandey of this institute for his constant encouragement and support. I would like to acknowledge particularly Prof. R.J. Singh, Ex. Vice Chancellor, M.G. Kashi Vidyapith, Varanasi for inspiring me to complete this book. I am really greatful to him for his kind acceptance to bless me through the foreword of the book. The entire work is dedicated to Prof. K.P. Pandey, Ex. Vice Chancellor, M.G. Kashi Vidyapith and Director, SHEPA, Varanasi who inspired and encouraged me directly and indirectly. I have great pleasure in expressing my sincere thanks to all those teachers specially Prof. U.C. Vashishtha, Prof. Saroj Anand, Prof. Akhilesh Chaube, Prof. M. Varma, Dr. Anil Shukla and Dr. Tripta Trivedi, individuals specially Prof. B.D. Singh, Prof. H.C.S. Rathore, Prof. P.C. Shukla, Dr. Sunil Kumar Singh and Dr. Madhu kushwaha, colleagues specially Dr. J.P. Srivastava, Dr. M.L. Tripathi, Mr. K.M. Rakesh and Ms. Tulika, institutions and sources whose help and co-operation have made it possible to undertake and complete this book. I would also like to acknowledge Gyan Publishing House, New Delhi for publication of this book. Lastly, I wish to put on records the help, co-operation and inspiration that came from my wife Dr. Sunita Singh. Any suggestions for the improvement of this book will be highly appreciated.

April 27, 2009 **Vinod Kumar Singh**
Abshay Tritiya
(Vaishakh Shukla Tritiya)
Varanasi

1

Primary School Teachers and Teaching Competency

1.1 INTRODUCTION

Education is a process of human enlightenment and empowerment for the achievement of a better and higher quality of life. A sound and effective system of education results in the unfoldment of learners' potentialities, enlargement of their competencies and transformation of their interests, attitudes and values.

Recognizing such an enormous potential of education, all progressive societies have committed themselves to the universalisation of elementary education with an explicit aim of providing 'Quality Education for All'. They have also recognized the significance of expansion of secondary education, gradually reaching to a near universalisation level and simultaneously improving its quality for effective empowerment of as many more learners as possible in order to achieve advancements in socio-economic and other domains of life. While higher education has also great potential in this respect, it can generally be made accessible to only a small section of the society. But school education should be provided in the present times to practically all members of the society and therefore, its quality and efficiency assume special significance within the larger framework of personal, social and national development.

In this context, effective teacher education has a crucial role to play. In fact, it becomes a core condition to ensure high proficiency and quality of school education. In other words, effective school education anticipates effective teacher education.

Teachers can act as trail – blazers in the lives of learners and in the process of education for development. If teachers acquire professional competencies and commitment, and if they are enabled and empowered to perform their multiple tasks in the classroom as well as in the school and the community in a genuinely professional manner, then a chain reaction can begin – starting with a sound teacher performance culminating into a high quality learning among increasingly more students in cognitive, affective and psychomotor areas of human development.

It is a universally acknowledged fact that an educated and enlightened citizen is an essential condition for the successful functioning of a democracy. Education at least up to the elementary level, is considered essential for every individual in a democratic country. When our country became free in 1947, education in India had to meet the changes taking place in the country and its need and aspirations. As far as possible, educational changes should be based on indigenous thinking, with suitable adaptation of ideas and models developed and tried out elsewhere. Hence the newly born free nation had to develop a system of education to meet its own specific needs.

Universal primary education was the first and foremost demand of independent India. It was felt that the state should provide free and compulsory education to all children till they reached the age of 14 years – a demand persistently ignored by the British government on one pretext or the other. This idea found a place in the constitution as a directive principle of State Policy (Article 45) and the country was obliged to set the target of cent per cent elementary education of the age group 6-14 within a period of ten years from the adoption of the constitution. But it has not been fulfilled even after six decades.

A number of factors responsible for the poor performance in this regard have been identified. Lack of finance and facilities, unsuitable curriculum, and parental apathy are among others, the main factors coming in the way of universal primary education in India.

Another problem of education in India concerns the provision of a growing number of qualified and professionally competent teachers through whom alone can the true objectives of education be realized. What is necessary here is to broaden our conception of the education of teachers? The training of a teacher should equip him to see and perform his role as a part, however humble, of the total endeavour of national reconstruction.

Primary education (or 'basic' education as Mahatma Gandhi suggested), caters to the most fundamental need of all men and is something that men cannot do without. It is the right to such education that the universal declaration of human rights mention as a human rights.

Literacy does not stop with acquiring the three R's but goes further in developing the innate talents of children. Both qualitative and quantitative aspects of education, especially in a densely populated country like India, should get equal stress in all the efforts.

Children have to be moulded and guided for proper development of their innate talents and for that purpose; the teacher must possess the required competencies, skills and the bent of mind.

Of the many projects implemented with the aim of achieving UPE through improving teacher competencies and skills, the innovative and home grown District Primary Education Programme (DPEP) is the latest.

A lot of research/ survey work has preceded the launch of this holistic programme. Further research on the effects, outcomes of this comprehensive national programme is indispensable for chalking out further strategies to achieve the cherished goal of UPE.

There was a time, especially during the pre-independence period in India, when teacher education was just a single-shot event. But this once-in – a lifetime model is quite inadequate in the post-independence period, particularly in the modern times. In the last decades of the twentieth century, both school education and society have witnessed unprecedented technological advancements, communication revolutions, periodical reforms in school curriculum, introduction of competency-based and value – oriented education, adoption of Minimum Levels of Learning (MLL) strategy as envisaged by National Policy on Education (NPE), 1986 (modified 1992), major reforms in textbooks - cum – workbooks and other teaching–learning aids, promoting activity-based and joyful learning, introduction of self-learning and group learning activities besides teacher-directed learning, offering non-formal and alternative education systems, initiatives like Operation Blackboard (OB), Special Orientation Programme for Teachers (SOPT), Promoting Primary and Elementary Education (PROPEL) and a host of other developments.

Clearly, all these and many other changes occurring in quick succession in school and society, coupled with new challenges to be faced in the initial decades of the twenty-first century, which also marks the dawn of a third millennium, have profound implications for the renewal of curricula, content and processes of teacher education. If teacher education has to remain effective and functional, its curriculum and related aspects should be revamped and renewed urgently. What is more, effective teacher education for elementary stage of education has now to be conceived with a more comprehensive paradigm encompassing a number of inter-related components.

1.2 CONCEPTUAL FRAMEWORK

1.2.1 Competency

Competence is nothing more than an improved modern term applied to an ancient human value; for example, the right way of doing things is the competent way, the right way to perform a job, the right way to live and work in association and cooperation with others. In other words, it means a desired quality of job performance. The qualities of competency are enthusiasm, fluency, industry, neatness, originality, adaptability and thrift. The training for competency has always been and still is largely training for creating abilities or qualities that are placed in actual job situation/ context. Competence does not result from possession of great amount of knowledge. It must become functionally operative at the appropriate time. Knowledge must be integrated into a pattern of behaviour to serve a useful purpose.

Applied to teachers, competency means the right way of conveying units of knowledge, application and skills to the students. The right way includes knowledge of contents as well as the processes, methods and means of conveying them in an interesting way, involving the activities of students. In short, a competent teacher makes the teaching-learning process a joyous experience for children and also to himself/ herself.

Competency can be described as a set of knowledge, skills, abilities and behavioural attributes which are required to deliver superior performance in a job position. Competency development and training generally go hand in hand. The organization, which gives priority to building and developing competencies of people, gives priority to training. Similarly, the organization, which gives priority to training, conducts the training with good intentions, continuously to build and rebuild, tune and fine-tune competencies. Competency development must be a continuous process in the organization. The training programmes instituted in organizations must address ways and means of effectively building competencies of people of the organization. A clear understanding of the process of competency development will help the organizations to impart training effectively.

Thus, competency encompasses many identifiable individual behaviours or skills that can be specified in behavioural term and recommends the observable demonstration of a composite of the specific skills and knowledge. The learning of large list of individual skills is a little value unless these skills can be combined and interrelated so that with practice they result in a capability for a composite performance, which is greater than the sum of the parts. A competency statement, thus, is a description of those performances that are based on the acquisition, integration, composite building and application of a set of related skill and knowledge. These performances entail a growth process, gestalt building as well as learning of individual skills.

1.2.2 Teaching Competency

Teaching competency can be defined as identifiable effective teaching behaviours or composite skills that are required for the transaction of the content and can be specified in behavioural term, which is aimed to bring about desired pupil outcomes and which are fairly demonstrable. It can be said that teaching process is determined by knowledge, a set of abilities, attitudes and skills which in turn determine pupil outcomes. So the term teaching can be understood as a set of observable teacher behaviour that facilitate or bring about pupil learning and teaching competency means an effective performance of all the observable teacher behaviours that bring about desired pupil outcomes.

1.2.3 Dictionary Meaning

To explain competency in precise terms the dictionary meanings and definitions are presented below:

According to **International Dictionary of Education (1978),** Competence means "the need for the child to show an ability to handle his/her environment and control his / her experience within it."

Competency based education course or programme is "one which trains and tests education students in stated skills in actual and simulated teaching situations."

A Dictionary of Education (1981) conceived competency based teaching as that movement within Teacher Education whose proponents "trained teachers in specific skills of interacting with pupils in classroom and who advocate that courses taken by prospective and in service teachers should spell out very clearly the knowledge, skills and attitudes they are expected to acquire."

The International Encyclopedia of Education (1985) gives several meanings of competence such as "adequate for the purpose, suitable, sufficient", "legally qualified, admissible" and "capable". In a sense it refers to adequate preparation to begin a professional career and has a direct linkage to certification requirements.

The meaning of competence given in **Webster's Third New International Dictionary (1964)** is "the quality or state of being functionally adequate or of having sufficient knowledge, judgment, skill or strength."

According to **Dictionary of Education (1997),** Competency Based Education is "an educational approach based on a predetermined set of knowledge, skills and abilities that the student is expected to accomplish..... It concerns about school accountability."

By competency based teacher education is meant, "a program of study for teacher preparation that is designed on the basis of a predetermined set of outcomes that is usually related to particular skills, knowledge and attitudes. The program requires the demonstration of specific competencies for completion."

According to **Encyclopedia Dictionary of Education (1997),** competence means as "the state of having and demonstrating skills, abilities or aptitudes in the satisfactory execution of a learning task."

Competency based education is a (1) system used in elementary and secondary schooling that features the detailed definition, teaching and demonstration by students of those competencies (involving knowledge, skills and behaviour) that have been defined as being of central importance. (2) any similar instructional system in employee training, education for a professional continuing education or other area.

1.2.4 Definitions

Hall and Jones (1976) define competencies as "composite skills, behaviours, or knowledge that can be demonstrated by the learner and are desired from explicit conceptualizations of the desired outcomes of learning. Competencies are states so as to make possible the assessment of student learning through direct observation of student behaviour."

Rama (1979) defines teacher competency as "the ability of a teacher manifested through a set of overt teacher classroom behaviours which is resulted of the interaction between the presage and product variables of teaching within a social setting."

Walker (1992), developed the following definition of competence, "the attributes (knowledge, skill, attitudes) which enable an individual or group to perform a role or set of tasks to an appropriate level or grade of quality or achievement (i.e. an appropriate standard) and thus make the individual of group competent in that role."

Barbara and Field (1994), defined competencies as "the types of skills, knowledge and attitudes that will form the basis of effective professional practice."

Thus the term 'Competence' can be understood as "quality or state of having and demonstrating skills, knowledge, attitudes and aptitudes while executing a task", and the 'teaching competency' can be conceived as "a professional ability of teachers to meet the set standards of efficiency in terms of knowledge, skill and attitudes in teaching learning process."

1.3 CLASSIFICATION OF TEACHER COMPETENCIES

The teacher has a role to play as a friend, philosopher and guide and secure the cooperation of society, co-workers, officials and so on in the discharge of his /her duties and for the achievement of the designed results. As such the competencies can be classified as under:

1.3.1 Classification 1

According to **Borich and Fenton (1977),** there are three types of teacher competencies:

1. Knowledge Competencies

Knowledge competencies specify the cognitive understanding a teacher is expected to demonstrate. Knowledge competencies can be achieved either from process of teaching or from content of the subject. By process of teaching is meant ability of teacher to give methods of managing the classroom effectively. While content of subject means knowledge of a particular subject. Both the above types of knowledge competencies can be measured directly by paper and pencil methods or indirectly by observing the teaching performance.

2. Performance Competencies

By performance competencies is meant the ongoing teaching behaviours performed in the classroom. Performance competencies require appropriate assessment methods, as these competencies deal with classroom processes. There is no consensus of instrument is used to measure such behaviours as the teacher's ability to ask higher order cognitive questions to demonstrate enthusiasm, using direct and indirect questioning techniques, enquiring pupil responses, accepting pupil feelings. Knowledge of these behaviours is pre-requisite for their execution. Assessment of this knowledge is not sufficient evidence of teachers' competence for actual performance of these behaviors. Thus, to measure performance competencies, systematic observations of classroom behaviours are most appropriate.

3. Consequence Competencies

Consequence Competencies specify pupil behaviours that are viewed as evidence of teaching effectiveness. Consequence competencies come under the ultimate level of competence receiving most attention. These competencies refer to pupil outcomes produced by the proper use of knowledge and performance competencies by the teacher. Like knowledge competencies both content and process behaviours can be specified. Content related behaviours involve the pupil's mastery over the subject matter. Process related competencies refer to emotions and attitudes of pupils which are affected by the classroom teachers. Process type consequence competencies can be measured by observing classroom behaviours of pupils.

1.3.2 Classification 2

According to Rao (1998), competencies can be classified as under:

1. **Performance based Competencies:** Learner demonstrates that he/she can perform some activity rather than simply being aware of facts. Performance based competencies are skill based and overt action oriental.
2. **Consequence based Competencies:** To demonstrate this competency a person is required to bring a change in others. The level of success is not measured by what one knows or does but by what one accomplishes. The achievement of pupils is a standard measure of consequence based competency.
3. **Affective Competency:** A great emphasis has to be laid on this type of competency rather than the previous categories. What one know is not important but what one is able to teach and so bring a change in the pupils is important. The affective competencies define the expected attitudes and values and tend to resist specificity. These competencies are expressed in terms of behaviour rather than by precept.
4. **Exploratory competencies:** This type of competencies is those that cannot be fitted into any of the above four types in competency based teacher education. The activities provide opportunity to students to learn, but specific nature of outcome cannot be desired. They are also referred as experience objective or expressive objectives.

1.3.3 Classification 3

Bara and Field (1994) listed competencies for beginning teachers. They classified competencies into two types:

A. Generic Competencies

B. Specific Competencies

A. Generic Competencies

The various lists of competencies for beginning teachers that have been produced by government bodies are of necessity of generic competencies. It implies that the skills and competencies apply in all settings and contexts, at all levels and to all modes of teaching. These competencies are meant to apply to all beginning teachers from early childhood teachers to senior secondary teachers. There are core skills, which are required in competent teaching irrespective of subject content, student's characteristics and specific school context. Teaching is a complex process and that sensible judgments cannot be made about a teacher's attainment of any competence without taking into account the social context, the individual characteristics of the teacher and the nature of the students to be taught. Competencies considered important enough to be included are usually demonstrable or at least observable. If they can not be operationalized or observed it becomes very difficult to assess them objectively. Most Higher Education Institutions with a program of Initial Teacher Education would have in their guides for supervising teachers, a list of generic competencies expected of the student teacher. Major generic competencies are given below:

1. Relationships with pupils (in both the pastoral and the teaching context)
2. Subject knowledge (students' competence in their own field of knowledge)
3. Planning (preparing individual lessons and curriculum units)

4. Class Management (organizing the learning enrichment)
5. Communication
6. Assessment (Assessing, recording and interpreting pupil performance)
7. Reflecting on practice (Evaluating one's own teaching and modifying professional practice)
8. Professionalism (setting and maintaining appropriate standards of professional behaviour)
9. Personal qualities

B. Specific Competencies

Specific competencies are those that apply to the specific subject areas in curriculum. These are being researched by subject specialists.

1.3.4 Classification 4

Goel et. al. (2000)

Involvement of Primary School Teachers in Academic and Non-Academic Activities

A discrepancy has been found between competencies expected and competencies in practice among the primary school teachers. 22 out of 57 expected competencies mainly related to teaching are not in practice (Bawane, J., 1999). The teachers are more involved in non-academic activities, such as, census data collection, elections and social service activities. The balance between the non academic and academic activities can be realized by developing the desired competencies among the primary school teachers (Table 1 and 2 present the competencies in practice and competencies not in practice).

Table 1.1. Comprehensive List of Competencies Identified as in Practice among Primary School Teachers

Sl. No.	*Competency*
1.	Plan the lessons
2.	Utilize textbooks and manuals
3.	Identify student learning needs and interests
4.	Motivate the students
5.	Utilize the blackboard
6.	Utilize the technique of questioning
7.	Communicate effectively
8.	Recite poems
9.	Narrate stories
10.	Conduct dramatization
11.	Conduct role play
12.	Provide experience based teaching
13.	Establish rapport with the students
14.	Promote student participation
15.	Manage the classroom discipline
16.	Manage the learning environment
17.	Conduct oral-drill exercises
18.	Utilize the community resources
19.	Summarize the lessons
20.	Assign homework
21.	Adopt play-way method
22.	Adopt self instruction technique
23.	Construct appropriate evaluation tools
24.	Conduct continuous and comprehensive evaluation
25.	Assess students in cultural activities

Sl. No.	*Competency*
26.	Involve students in cultural activities
27.	Arrange outdoor activities (Visits/trips)
28.	Conduct sports and games
29.	Develop institutional plans
30.	Assist in maintaining records
31.	Work in a team of colleagues
32.	Establish rapport with staff
33.	Undertake self evaluation
34.	Assist in conducting surveys
35.	Participate in social service activities

Table 1.2. List of Competencies Not-Practiced According to Majority of the Primary School Teachers

Sl. No.	*Competency*
1.	Prepare teaching aids
2.	Utilizing teaching aids
3.	Operate hardware (T.V., Radio)
4.	Demonstrate experiments
5.	Adopt concept attainment approach
6.	Adopt project method
7.	Adopt guided discovery method
8.	Adopt inductive-deductive method
9.	Adopt problem solving method
10.	Adopt creative teaching method
11.	Adopt group discussion method
12.	Provide effective feedback
13.	Diagnose student learning difficulties

Sl. No.	*Competency*
14.	Organize remedial instruction
15.	Provide educational assistance for children with special needs
16.	Undertake multigrade teaching
17.	Organize and conduct guidance activities
18.	Conduct follow up activities
19.	Conduct action research
20.	Implement new educational ideas
21.	Analyze a textbook
22.	Establish rapport with parents and community

1.3.5 Classification 5

Rao (1998)

Teacher Competencies in Relation to Raising Achievement Level

I. Class Related Competencies

1. Lesson Planning and Instructional Management
2. Evaluating and Remedial Skill
3. Innovating and Experimenting.

II. School Related Competencies

4. Development of Positive Attitudes
5. Administration and Management
6. Inter-school Relations
7. Image and Morale Building.

III. Pupil Related Competencies

8. Identification of Pupils Talents

9. Identification of Pupils' Characteristics
10. Identification of Pupils' Needs
11. Developing Non-Cognitive Skills among Pupils
12. Guidance and Counseling Skills
13. Helping Pupils to Develop Personality

IV. Community Related Competencies

14. Awareness Building
15. Ensuring Building
16. Mobilization of Resources and its Utilisation
17. Public Relations

V. Curriculum

18. Initiating
19. Planning
20. Developing
21. Implementing
22. Evaluating Skills

VI. Motivational Competencies

23. Motivating Pupils
24. Motivating Colleagues
25. Motivating the Society

VII. Value Related Competencies

26. Playing an Ethical Role Model
27. Developing Values Among Pupils
28. Developing Values among Members of the Society.

VIII. Leadership Role Model

29. Developing Leadership Qualities for Self

30. Developing Leadership Qualities among Colleagues
31. Developing Leadership Qualities among Students
32. Developing Leadership Qualities among Societal Members

1.3.6 Classification 6

In the consultations initiated by NCTE (1998) at several national seminars, the following ten inter –related categories of competencies have emerged quite prominently:

1. Contextual competencies;
2. Conceptual competencies;
3. Content competencies;
4. Transactional competencies;
5. Competencies related to other educational activities;
6. Competencies to develop teaching –learning materials;
7. Evaluation competencies;
8. Management competencies;
9. Competencies related to working with parents; and
10. Competencies related to working with community and other agencies.

1.3.6.1 Contextual Competencies

One of the first and foremost obligations of primary school teachers is to ensure acceptability of their efforts by the parents and the community. Towards this, they need to acquire a near total understanding of the socio-economic, cultural, linguistic and religious contexts of the specific family milieu and the community profile. Policy provisions for equality, social justice, educational opportunity etc. will also have to be understood both in the form of written statements as also in pragmatic terms of their appreciation by the concerned community. The teachers' job is thus an integral part not only of the total educational system but also of the total social and cultural systems in which they have to operate. They must, therefore, be fully familiar with the education systems at the National and State levels well as with their global and local ramifications. They should be able to identify and analyze the factors responsible for obstructing the growth of literacy in the country and the concerned State, besides reasons for poor enrolment, retention and the problems of wastage and stagnation in the schools. They have also to understand the heterogeneities and diversities of the society while working out unifying factors for building a cohesive society that believes in national integration and attempt to provide every citizen a sense of belonging to the nation with dignity and equality. They will also have to understand various other issues like developmental activities, urbanization, unemployment, value inculcation, political dynamics and the growing impact of scientific and technological development etc. against the backdrop of the specific community. To ensure credibility of their actions and initiatives, their preparation, based primarily on the afore-said considerations, has to be a pre-requisite for the teachers. They have to be alive to contexts like these and develop, in turn, relevant competencies and corresponding skills. The existing curriculum could be explored for such components as could be converted into competencies. The gaps, if any, could also be identified and filled by working out suitable measures and developing workable strategies.

1.3.6.2 Conceptual Competencies

It is a quality essential to develop in the student teachers the right perspective in education that would enable them to receive new experiences meaningfully and in greater detail and depth, besides helping them thoroughly understand the meaning of education and learning and the impact of socio-economic and socio-cultural factors on them. They should also know their educational implications with reference to the physical, mental, social and cultural needs of the child at different stages of child development. It is, therefore, imperative for the teachers to know significant characteristics of child development at different age levels to enable them to translate these characteristics into curriculum transactions including practical work. The knowledge of sociometry of the class too would help them organize curricular and co-curricular activities quite effectively in the classroom and outside. This would also help them adopt various modalities of curriculum transaction such as teacher directed learning, group learning, self-motivated individualized learning and the like.

1.3.6.3 Content Competencies

Needless to say that the teachers should achieve full mastery over the content competencies identified in the competency based curriculum of primary schools. It gains all the more importance in the context of a study conducted in this area which revealed that 50% of the new entrants of teacher education institutions, who acquired more than 75% marks at the Senior School Certificate examinations, scored less than 30% marks in the content test based on the curriculum of primary school. In this light, it becomes essential that the content competencies, identified by Dave Committee Report or its adaptation by the State, must be achieved at the level of full mastery by the student teachers in their teacher preparation programmes at the Teacher Education Institutes. Besides, the student teachers must develop ability to analyse the existing curriculum content and co-relate it with relevant competencies. In this process, it should be possible for them to find out gaps and the hard spots of learning which often exist. They should also identify such areas from the curriculum where there is enough scope for joyful activities, individual learning and group learning. It could also be an enlightening experience to utilize media intervention for a high level of content enrichment of the learning teaching process that may also, in turn, facilitate the transactional strategies.

1.3.6.4 Transactional Competencies

Teaching – learning process in education involves interaction between the teacher and the taught resulting in the achievement of the desired competencies. Teaching as a concept is to be conceived in these stages: 1. planning, 2. teaching-learning process and 3. evaluation. During transaction, the teachers put plan into action and evaluate its impact in terms of competency achievement level at the end of the transaction. One of the important causative factors for poor achievement at the primary level is poor curriculum transaction. Acharya Ramamurti Committee Report, 1992 on National Policy on Education, 1986 revealed that the present teacher education programme, being mainly theory oriented, due emphasis is not being given on practice teaching. In fact, this lacuna has been repeatedly observed by various commissions. In that, the 1964-66 Commission treated practice teaching as the weakest link in the chain of the entire teacher education process and recommended its strengthening on top priority basis. Hence, it is imperative that student teachers need to be fully trained in this area.

In the competency based teaching-learning process, the subject content is used merely as a vehicle to achieve relevant identified competencies at the level of mastery. While transacting curriculum content, the principles of psychology, management and societal aspects, as the case may be, should be integrated and practiced, it becomes extremely important for the student teachers to understand clearly the process of child development and growth and the management principles involved in order to affect maximum learning by the child. This would also further facilitate the transactional strategies.

Since the young children have short span of attention, time for teacher-directed learning should be of fairly short span and in that, more time should be devoted to group learning and individualized self-learning by children themselves. It involves proper use of the textbooks so as to emphasize on the workbook reinforcement of the acquired competencies through direct involvement of the child.

1.3.6.5 Competencies Related to other Educational Activities

The curricular activities are supposed to take care of the cognitive development of the children. But these alone may be inadequate for their total development. Their development in the non-cognitive area is equally important, which deserves due consideration as part of their learning –teaching process and transactional strategies.

Human values are imbibed by children naturally and spontaneously through participation in educational activities such as morning prayer/assembly; celebration of national events like Independence Day, Republic Day, Children's Day, Teacher's Day, Birth Centenary of national leaders, celebration of social and cultural events like Janmashtami, Navaratra, Ganesh Mahotsav, Diwali, Eid, Christmas, Mahavir Jayanti, Budda Jayanti, Guru Nanak Jayanti; community life activities like Gram-safai, Eye-camp, Polio campaign, Excursions, Dramas; interaction of children with creative individuals who have attained distinction in life and the like.

1.3.6.6 Competencies to Develop Teaching-learning Material

Developments of competencies need different kinds of teaching-learning material. Without a strong input of the self-learning material, competencies at mastery level may not be achieved by the learners. Some of these materials such as textbooks, workbooks etc. for initial teaching of new competencies and in the form of different lessons have to be prepared and brought out. Textual material should also be prepared for generating group interaction and inter-learning by organizing learning in groups. Besides, self-learning materials need also to be developed for ensuring quality by individualizing learning irrespective of class size and quantity in terms of meeting the learning needs of every learner. Workbooks can also help in the management of multigrade classroom situations which many teachers will be facing for quite some time in the future.

The teachers handbooks and similar other reading materials should be used by the teachers in order not only to maintain but also to improve their own professional standards. The classical teaching learning aids such as pictures, charts, maps, diagrams, tables, models etc. should be prepared, selected and used by the teachers to enrich the quality of their teaching still further.

Teaching –learning materials based on new technology such as audio tapes, video tapes, slides, radio, T.V., computer and similar other gadgets should also be used by the teachers to make their teaching effective and lasting. In addition, specially designed materials should be prepared and used for remedial as well as enrichment of individual children of small groups. These should be based on the diagnosis of their individual strengths and weaknesses in terms of achievement in a given classroom.

Teachers should also make use of locally available learning resources such as bank, post-office, hospital, ONGC centre, PCO booth etc. to enrich their learning teaching experiences.

1.3.6.7 Evaluation Competencies

In the new approach, towards introducing competency based curriculum, the competency based evaluation system should be adopted. As the entire programme is oriented to the quantitative as well as qualitative achievement of the learner, training should be modified and geared to an improvement oriented evaluation approach rather than the measurement oriented or impersonal approach to evaluation. In order to follow this type of positivistic evaluation as against the negativistic which evolves fear, contempt, a new set of concept should be developed in the teachers.

1.3.6.8 Management Competencies

Every teacher is a manager of a particular class or group of students. As such the teachers should be taught the required skills of classroom management including total teaching as well as subject teaching in the class, and several other tasks expected of them in and outside the school. These competencies and qualities, required for effective maintenance and management, are to be inculcated among the student teachers during their training period. They have also to be responsible with other teachers and the Headmaster at school level which demands that they should not only be taught their relative roles and responsibilities as individual teachers but also as responsible partners in managing the school affairs to optimize the learning – teaching outcomes of the school.

1.3.6.9 Competencies Related to Working with Parents

The most critical issue in elementary education is the universalisation of elementary education. The target groups now are dropouts and unenrolled children. In both the cases, the role of parents is quite crucial. In the past, it was not given due consideration, but presently it has become extremely important on various counts.

In different areas where parental contexts are quite needed and the teachers will have to have a new type of commitment to deal with them. As such, these areas of parents' co-operation in the learning-teaching process are required to be adequately incorporated in teacher education programmes to develop related competencies among the student teachers during their preparation as teachers.

1.3.6.10 Competencies Related to Working with Community and other Agencies

To improve the school situation, the teachers have to seek co-operation of members of the community as well. This point was neglected during the colonial period as the then administrators preferred to keep the schools segregated and separated from the community. No school can function in isolation and, therefore, the teacher should work towards bringing the school and the community as close as possible and inter-related. For this purpose, some kind of a professionally systematic orientation is needed. The teachers should understand the role of the community in the development of the school and should analyze how best the local agencies can contribute to various school purposes.

Teachers now have a challenging task. They need to develop competencies to be acceptable to the community and, in turn, be able to ensure community support for the school. For this, the teachers should be made competent in activities like community survey, school mapping etc. Facilitating pupils' learning is, no doubt, an important function of teachers. This can be performed effectively only when the teachers get the required support from local people and as such they need to identify local resources to augment the possibility of community support for educational purposes and quality school education.

After study of all types of competencies mentioned above, the researcher decided to measure following five types of competencies of primary school teachers:

1. Competencies related to other educational activities
2. Contextual competencies
3. Transactional Competencies
4. Content competencies
5. Competencies to develop teaching learning material

1.4 EMERGENCE OF THE PROBLEM

Education, in general, and primary education in particular, is an essential input in the process of national development. Primary education is that crucial stage of education which lays the foundation of later development. Good primary education requires good teachers. It demands teachers who are of high moral caliber and possess competencies of high level. It was stated in Education Commission (1964-66) that "of all the factors that influence the quality of education the competence and character of teacher are undoubtedly the most significant."

The progress made in the provision of schooling facilities has been quite impressive, but mere existence of schooling facility does not guarantee the participation of children in schools. Government data reveals that nearly 5.49 lakh students in the age group of 6 to 14 are out of schools. Those, who are enrolled, do not complete the full cycle of primary education. The dropout rate at primary level is around 40.1%, in U.P., while at upper primary level it is around 54% (Year 2000 Assessment - Education For All). The vision on indicators of primary education has undergone great changes after the publication of the report of the World Conference on Education For All (WCEFA, Inter Agency Commission 1990).

In a paper 'Private School Allure' (2001) it is quoted that more than 93% of primary school children are enrolled in private schools in Lucknow city. Another study conducted on Lakhimpur Khiri district (2001) reveals that there is a long dissonance between the expectations of parents/children and the performance of primary school teachers. Such findings compel us to re-think about system of primary education because this is the area in which our Government is making all efforts not only by its own resources but also with international assistance to make available quality education to all.

When we talk about quality education (World Bank Report, 1998), a lot of responsibilities automatically come on the shoulders of teachers. In the 21st market oriented century, where any investment is made with the expectations of sufficient return, the cost – return ratio of primary education is quite pertinent.

In the Birla Ambani Report (1998) and WTO agreement, it has been argued that quality of primary education should be judged by the performance of primary school teachers in the context of responsibilities which are embedded with their profession.

In Delors' report (1996) it was advocated that competency based and commitment oriented education is needed to solve the tensions of coming century. Now question arises, what type of competencies are needed in a successful teacher? These may be in the form of content competencies, contextual competencies, performance-related competencies, etc. Recently, in a study of SCERT (UP) competencies were determined on the basis of Presage, Process and Product variables.

As admitted in the report of 'Education for All' and other studies to the best of the knowledge of the researcher, reliable and baseline studies are not available in respect to the above issues. This calls for an intensive, extensive and exhaustive study for providing data-base required to evolve strategies and guidelines that may help in overcoming the problem and bringing about improvements and marked changes in the teaching competencies of primary school teachers. Such a study will also give an opportunity to examine the relative contribution of each variable undertaken in the study to the competency of primary school teachers.

1.5 NEED AND JUSTIFICATION

There is a rivalry between parishadiya schools and private schools, where parishadiya schools are at the verge to loose the battle. Thus, there is a need to identify less competent teachers. Government is making nearly 50% expenditure on primary education of total budget allotted to education. Thus it is expected that this expenditure would create a conducive environment for quality education. These dreams would not convert into reality if teachers of the system are not competent. Performance-linked pay scales have been introduced successfully in many public sector setting (like Tata, Reliance). In coming years, it may be introduced in education sector too. This study will give us a platform to see the performance of teachers on selected indicators. Quality indicators are necessary to control the system. Thus the development of quality indicators on the basis of performance of teachers in this study is quite pertinent. As per the requirement of local conditions, no standardized and academically accepted tool is available to measure the competencies of primary teachers. This need advocates for the construction of a reliable and valid tool which the present study is to do.

There are very few studies conducted in India and other countries. Whatever studies are available related to this area reveals that evidence in this regard is not comprehensive. The study is important from both, the educational and the sociological points of view.

1.6 STATEMENT OF THE PROBLEM

In light of the need and justification of the study, the statement of the problem related to this research work was formally stated as 'A Study of Teaching Competencies of Primary School Teachers in relation to Gender, Academic Qualification and Habitat'.

1.7 OBJECTIVES

The present study was undertaken with a view to achieve the following objectives –

1. To find out the level of competencies of primary school teachers working in Lucknow city.
2. To compare the teaching competency of Primary School Teachers with respect to their Gender.
3. To compare the teaching competency of Primary School Teachers with respect to their Academic Qualification.
4. To compare the teaching competency of Primary School Teachers with respect to their Professional Training.
5. To compare the teaching competency of Primary School Teachers with respect to their Habitat.
6. To compare the teaching competency of Primary School Teachers with respect to Teaching Experience.
7. To compare the teaching competency of Primary School Teachers with respect to Academic Stream i.e. Science, Arts and Commerce.

1.8 HYPOTHESES

To arrive at meaningful conclusions and to achieve the above mentioned objectives of the study, the researcher has tried to use as much rigorous design as possible. As the study is exploratory in nature, therefore the following hypotheses were formulated for identifying the effect of various factors on the teaching competencies of primary school teachers of Lucknow District.

H_1 — Majority of Primary School Teachers will be found to possess 'high'/'very high' level of Teaching Competency.

H_2 — There is no significant difference in mean scores of teaching competency of primary school teachers with respect to their gender.

H_3 — There is no significant difference in mean scores of teaching competency of primary school teachers with respect to their academic qualification.

H_4 — There is no significant difference in mean scores of teaching competency of primary school teachers with respect to their training.

H_5 — There is no significant difference in mean scores of teaching competency of primary school teachers with respect to their habitat.

H_6 — There is no significant difference in mean scores of teaching competency of primary school teachers with respect to their teaching experience.

H_7 — There is no significant difference in mean scores of teaching competency of primary school teachers with respect to their academic stream.

1.9 OPERATIONAL DEFINION OF THE TERMS USED

1.9.1 Teaching Competency

Teaching competency in the present study includes the acquisition and demonstration of the composite skills required for student teaching like introducing a lesson, fluency in questioning, probing questioning, explaining, stimulus variation, silence and non verbal cues, pacing the lesson, using audio-visual aids, illustrating with examples, using blackboard, reinforcement, understanding child psychology, recognizing attending behaviour, classroom management and giving assignment.

1.9.2 Primary School Teacher

There are so many grades of schooling. Among them the primary grade of teaching-learning process is one which runs from class I to V. In this study the term primary school teacher denotes the teachers who teach primary classes, i.e. I to V.

1.9.3 Academic Qualification

Academic qualification refers to the level of education attained by primary school teachers, e.g. High School, Intermediate, Graduation, etc.

1.9.4 Gender

Gender indicates whether the teacher is male or female.

1.9.5 Habitat

Habitat means living location of the person concerned i.e. Rural and Urban. Rural means born and brought up in village. Urban means born and brought up in town or city.

1.10 DELIMITATION OF THE STUDY

1. The study is confined to Primary School Teachers of Lucknow District only.
2. The study has been confined to 4 blocks only. 2 blocks namely, Mall and Bakshi Ka Talab, from rural areas and 2 blocks/wards namely, Sahadatganj and Valdi Ka Khera, from urban areas.
3. Only a few demographic variables namely gender, academic qualification, training, habitat, teaching experience and academic stream were selected for the study. The study of other variables was dropped due to shortage of time and information.
4. The study is delimited to a sample of 200 teachers only.

1.11 ORGANIZATION OF THE BOOK

This book is prepared, systematically, in five chapters under appropriate headings as shown below. The chapters are followed by appendix and bibliography.

Chapter I : Primary School Teachers and Teaching Competency – In this chapter the background, conceptual framework, emergence of the problem, need and justification, statement of the problem, its objectives, hypotheses, operational definitions, delimitations of the study along with plan of the book have been discussed.

Chapter II : Studies Conducted in the Past – This chapter consists of review of related literature in the field of the study, summary of some of the relevant researches done in India and abroad on teaching competencies of primary school teachers related to academic qualification, gender, habitat and other variables have been included.

Chapter III : Design and Procedure of the Study – In this chapter the method adopted in the investigation of the problem has been discussed. It deals with methodology of research, sampling design, description of the research tools, their administration, nature of the test and statistical design.

Chapter IV : Results of the Study on Teaching Competency of Primary School Teachers – This chapter deals with data and their analysis, collected from self made tool administered on primary school teachers of Lucknow district.

Significant analysis and interpretation of the data with respect to the hypotheses and discussion of the result have also been discussed in the chapter.

Chapter V : Teaching Competency of Primary School Teachers – This chapter attempts to present the conclusions drawn, educational implications of the study and also suggestions for further researches.

Appendices

Bibliography

Subject Index

2

Studies Conducted in the Past

The survey of related literature is an important component of the planning of any research study. This chapter deals with the review of the research studies and the literature related to the present research problem. Review of the related literature is crucial pre-requisite to actual planning and execution of the research work. In a bid to keep the investigator abreast of the work already done on the subject, to acquaint him of the procedure adopted to explore the field, to avoid pitfalls of the past researches and the repetition of the field already covered, the researcher made a thorough search of the literature from Encyclopedia, Research abstracts, Journals and Books. In the following pages an attempt has been made to describe those studies which have adequate relevance to the present study.

At this stage it may also be noted that the present review can hardly be expected to provide the comprehensive picture of the researches related to teaching competency of primary school teachers. However, an attempt has been made to review and synthesize the available literature related to directly or indirectly with the theme of present study.

In order to make the presentation of related research studies systematic, all studies have been given year wise:

Avila (1979) examined the effects of selected teaching competencies on secondary students' achievement. The purpose was to determine whether specific teaching competencies applied in the classroom would increase students' learning.

The sample consisted of control and experimental teachers and students in English and Social Studies classes at the Secondary level. The data were analyzed by using statistical technique of analysis of covariance.

Selected findings of the study were (1) Through a staff development programme teachers can be taught to apply specific teaching competencies in the classroom. (2) Teaching competencies when properly applied in the classroom will significantly enhance the probability that students will learn. (3) Teachers can be trained to properly apply specific teaching competencies and the principles of learning in the classroom. (4) The planned and consistent use of teaching competencies can be uniformly effective in increasing the learning at three cognitive levels of knowledge, comprehension and application.

Sharma (1979) studied the development of teacher competencies of the B.Ed. student teachers in the training colleges of Rajasthan in relation to teacher behaviour characteristic.

The sample was drawn from three teachers' training colleges. In all, 350 B.Ed. student teachers were selected. The tools used were classroom observation record, socio-economic status scale, and teachers' behaviours characteristic scale. Factor Analysis, Analysis of Variance, Analysis of Covariance, t- test, Product- Moment Correlation and Multiple Regression analysis were used to analyse the data.

The main findings were (1) the development of competencies of the student teachers during the course of practice teaching was independent of their teaching experience, age, and socio-economic status and (2) sex, area of teaching experience (urban-rural), previous training, graduation from college or done privately and academic achievement of student teachers had no significant effect on the development of their competencies during practice teaching.

Watson (1979) tried to see the relationship of age, experience, degrees, prior positions and school size to competencies in seven selected job functions as perceived by principles of Indian Public Secondary Schools.

The field survey technique was adopted to obtain data. The sample consisted of 369 principals of public secondary schools. The research was based on responses to 27 questionnaire items received from principals. The data was expressed in number and percent and chi squares scores.

The study revealed that there is no relationship between the factors of age and school size and principals' perceptions of their competencies in the seven selected job functions.

Lalitha (1981) studied the 'Effectiveness at a strategy of training of Integrating Teaching skills on teaching competence of student teacher'. Finding was no significant difference between the two treatment groups after training for integration of teaching skills in simulated conditions in term of teaching competence measured on both G.T.C.S. and Indore Teaching Competence Scale Adjusted for initial difference in teacher attitude and pre performance on General Teaching Competence Scale and Indore Teaching Competence Scale.

Joshi and Kumar (1983) examined the effect of the skills based approach and decision making ability on the development of teaching competence among teacher-trainees.

The study aimed at finding out the relative effect of teaching of two skill-based approaches on the development of teaching competence. A purposive sample of 22 B.Ed. students was selected and the data were collected with the help of an Observation Schedule, for measuring various skill developed by Joshi, Lalita and Passi.

The findings indicated that the mean performance was significantly higher in case of the group where the number of skills, time duration and number of pupils gradually increased in the light of their teaching competency scores as against the groups where all the skills were taken together.

Warren (1985) conducted a study to examine the relationships between the classroom teaching competencies of elementary school mathematics teachers and cognitive achievement in mathematics for third, fourth and fifth grade elementary school students across high and low socio-economic status (SES) settings.

The sample of the study consisted of 25 elementary school mathematics teachers. The data were collected by using the school system criterion- referenced mathematics tests. Pearson Product Moment coefficients of correlation, Multiple Regression and Analysis of variance were used to analyse the data.

The results supported the validity of the Teacher Performance Observation Record with one significant indicator behaviour for all teachers 'Uses time efficiently', 'Demonstrates patience, empathy, and understanding' and 'Manages disruptive behaviour'. Three indicators involving use of materials, structuring and warmth had significant inverse relationships to student percentage gain scores for both SES groups. The relationship between the number of instructional groups per classroom and student gain was slightly positive but not significant.

Prakasham (1986) studied the effect of school organizational climate on teacher effectiveness and teaching competency.

The sample of the study consisted of 800 teachers teaching in higher secondary school, along with 92 principals of these schools. The data were collected by employing the school Organization Climate Description, Questionnaire, the

General Teaching Competency Scale and the Teacher Effectiveness Scale. Mean, T Values, coefficient of correlation, ANOVA and F- ratios were computed for analyzing the data.

The findings of the study were (1) Teachers, working in an open school climate were better in teaching competency and teacher effectiveness than those employed in schools with autonomous, familiar, controlled paternal and closed climates. (2) Teachers working in schools situated in industrial area were found better in teaching competency than teachers working in semi-urban and rural areas whereas teachers of semi-urban and rural areas were better in teacher effectiveness than the teachers of industrial areas. However, teacher working in schools situated in urban areas were better than teachers of all other areas on both teaching competency as well as teachers' effectiveness. (3) A positive and significant relationship was observed in the teacher effectiveness and teaching competency of teachers in different types of organizational climates. (4) No significant difference was found in the teaching competency and teacher effectiveness of the teacher working in government and non-government schools in global terms. However teachers working in schools run by local bodies were found better in teaching competency.

Dave (1987) made a relative study of micro-teaching versus mini-teaching model in term of general teaching competence. It was conducted on student teachers. Finding was that the pupils liking of their teachers was not affected by variation of treatment of teacher preparation. Instead of the present training treatment given to teachers, some other personality factors might be influencing pupils liking of their teachers.

Anantha Krishnan (1988) conducted a study to find out the personal qualities, educational qualifications, and socio-economic background of B.Ed. students of Poona City.

The researcher tried to examine the different issues related to the teacher's training course. The aim of the study was to study the socio-economic, academic and personal background of B.Ed. students and also to find out their attitude towards teaching as well as methods of teaching. Random sampling method was used. The findings showed that female students showed more inclination towards B.Ed. course than male students.

Barnes L.R. and Shinn-Taylor C. (1988) studied teacher competency and primary school curriculum: a survey of five schools in North-East England.

An investigation into teacher competency and teacher expertise in five primary schools was undertaken by questionnaire and interview with 50 staff and five head teachers. Following a comparative review of all curriculum areas, two subjects are identified as giving serious cause for concern – music and science and these are given more detailed reporting. The data are compared with other research reports and the conclusion drawn that this investigation reinforces and extends existing literature on the limitations of teacher competency in primary schools. By a more flexible use of teacher expertise it is possible and indeed necessary and desirable, to use teachers in a specialist capacity to cover gaps in class teacher knowledge skills and interests.

Nelson (1988) tried to analyse the relationships between teacher competency and pupil achievement.

The objective of the study was to determine the relationship between the allocation of pupils to teachers of varying competencies and its effect on pupil achievement. The level of competency of the teacher, the students' gender, percentage of attendance and initial achievement level differences on the third grade CAT pretest scores were the independent variables against which the dependent variables of the fourth grade CAT post test scores in reading and mathematics were compared. An analysis of covariance, a two way analysis of variance, and the interaction between dimensions were used to analyse the data.

The findings revealed that the competency of the teacher did affect the achievement of pupils in reading and mathematics. Pupil attendance, gender and initial achievement level were found to have relatively no significant effect on students' achievement as they relate to teacher competency. Students in classrooms of 'poor teachers' regressed in reading, students in 'outstanding teachers' exhibited significant gains in mathematics. Supervisor's ratings of teacher competency were found to be accurate. The conclusions indicated that teachers indeed do make a difference in pupil achievement.

Prakasham (1988) compared the strength of teacher effectiveness in various types of school organization climates as well as under different levels of teaching competency across sex differentiation and territorial variation.

The objectives of the study were (i) to compare the strength of teacher effectiveness in various types of school organizational climates as well as under different levels of teaching competency across sex differentiation and territorial variation, (ii) to estimate the relationship of school organizational climates and teaching competency to teacher effectiveness (iii) to study the relative effects of school organizational climates and teaching competency on teacher effectiveness.

The sample comprised 800 teachers from 120 government, local bodies, private, non-Christian and Christian schools of Raipur and Bilaspur Districts together with 92 principals. The researchers used the school organizational climate description questionnaire of Motilal Sharma, General Teaching Competency Scale (GTCS) of B.K. Passi and M.S. Lalitha, and Teacher Effectiveness Scale

(TES) of T. Kumar and D.N. Mutha. Mean, SD, 't' ratio, Pearson's product–moment, co-efficient of correlation and ANOVA were computed for treating the data.

The findings depicted that (i) the open school organizational climate positively affected both the teaching competency as well as teacher effectiveness. (ii) Female teachers scored invariably higher with insignificant difference in all types of schools, categorized in terms of territory, management –type and organizational climate (iii) moderately better teacher effectiveness was observed in schools under Christian Management (iv) there existed a significant relationship between teaching competency and teacher effectiveness (v) Teaching competency, school organizational climate yielded highly significant main effects.

Chaudhary (1989) took into consideration the rigidity and lack of variety in pre-service teachers training programmes which was according to micro teaching and the Herbartian steps. The objective was to study that whether the student teachers had indirectly learned the teaching skills during peer practice and whether there was any difference in their competency in various teaching skills at the time of teaching through the Concept Attainment Model (CAM) and teaching through Traditional Teaching (TT)? The sample included the student teacher of Adarsha College of Education and Research.

The result revealed no significant difference in the competency of student teachers in stating the aim whereas few of them showed improvement while teaching during traditional teaching and also they had improved in the skill of evaluation.

Singh (1989) analysed the relative effectiveness of two training strategies in developing teaching competence and attitude towards teaching among student teachers.

The sample comprised 34 B.Ed. students of School of Education. The tools used Included Attitude towards Teaching Inventory, Micro-Teaching Theory Check Up, Attitude towards Micro Teaching and Teaching Competence Scale.

The study revealed that both the training strategies were significantly effective in developing theoretical understanding of micro-teaching, general teaching competence and attitude towards teaching.

Chaudhury (1990) undertook an exploratory study to find out the impact of teachers' personality on competency in Advance Organizer Model and Inductive Thinking Model.

The sample comprised of 10 student teachers of B.Ed. They were all female in the age group of 20 to 25 years having science and mathematics as methods of teaching. The tools used were 16 PF test, Teaching Analysis Guide for Advance Organizer Model, Teaching Analysis Guide for Inductive Thinking Model and BGTC scale. The obtained scores were analyzed on the basis of the factors of 16 PF and its categorization.

No clear cut picture has emerged from the analysis of data indicating any differentiating effect of the personality traits on competency on either Advance Organizer Model (AOM) or Inductive Thinking Model (ITM). Also those scoring high on general teaching competency on AOM also scored high on general teaching competency on Inductive Thinking Model. It was concluded that personality traits as measured by 16 PF test did not indicate any relationship with competency and willingness in following a deductive or inductive approach to teaching.

Thamilmani (1990) conducted a study to assess the relationship between teacher competency and achievement of students.

The sample of the study included 450 students of standard IX and 50 science teachers from various higher secondary schools. The tools used were students' Ratings on Teaching Competency, Teacher Competence Self-Appraisal Scale and Students' Achievement Test. Pearson's product-moment correlation and 't' test were used for statistical analysis of the data.

The study revealed that the teacher competence of Science teachers was related to the academic achievement of high school students. Teaching Competency and Pupils' Achievement are closely related and the relationship between the two is positive.

Pandya (1991) studied the relative effectiveness of microteaching and the traditional technique of teacher training in the development of general teaching competence of the student teachers of secondary teachers' colleges. Out of 100 students- teachers, two groups of 15 each equated on intelligence and attitude towards teaching were formed. Mean, SD and 't' test were used to analyse the data. The study concluded that micro teaching approach was more effective than the traditional teaching approach in the development of general teaching competence.

Srinivas, V. (1992) studied the personality traits of primary school-teachers of Cuddalore Educational District in Tamil Nadu. He found that (1) Age, Sex, Experience and Community did not affect the attitude of teachers towards teaching. (2) Government school teachers differed from aided-school –teachers with regard to attitude towards teaching. (3) Significant difference existed in some traits between men and women teachers (Lack of empathy), Government school teachers and private school teachers (Empathy and neurotism), teachers from the forward and the backward scheduled class communities (Pessimism) and teachers having long and short period of service (Self-confidence, dogmatism and need for achievement).

Khantachvana (1994) emphasized basically on technical teachers of Bankok, Thailand, taking into consideration their perceptions of needed professional competencies. The instruments used in this study were based on the areas of 1. Knowledge, 2. Cognitive skills. 3. Experimental skills, 4. Attitude and 5. Teaching Skills. The study showed that all competency categories as perceived by the technical teachers to be of high importance.

Maddox (1994) examined teacher competencies needed by new secondary vocational instructors in Georgia. The aim of the study was to find out the importance of the 80 instructional competencies as found by new vocational instructors who have got through the new teacher institute (NTI) from 1989 through 1993. The study indicated that no statistically significant differences in the ratings of importance of the 80 instructional competencies taught in the NTI were found.

Naseema (1994) studied the teaching competence of physical science teachers in relation to their satisfaction in teaching.

The sample comprised of 150 physical science teachers from secondary schools. The data was collected by Teaching Competence Rating Scale, General Teaching Competency Scale, Job Satisfaction Questionnaire and School Organizational Climate Description Questionnaire. The collected data was treated by using percentages, Bi- serial coefficient of correlation, chi-square, Pearson's product moment of correlation and multiple regression analysis.

The major findings of the study were (1) 30.92 percent of physical science teachers differed in perceived teaching competence due to work (0.01), rewards (1.73), context of work (0.87), self (0.61), others (0.56) and total satisfaction (27.15). (2) 26.89 percent of physical science teachers differed in observed teaching competence. This was attributed to work (0.86), rewards (0.002), context of work (1.5), self (2.32), others (1.91) and total satisfaction (20.3).

Jablonski (1996) studied that how the cognitive skill, self-efficacy, basic teaching techniques, knowledge of teaching practices and working conditions during internship affect teaching performance in a causal model. This included and Instructional Training Laboratory (ITL) and a year long mentored teaching internship. The result showed that end of year productive teaching activity directly affected self-efficacy. Knowledge of teaching practices also directly affected summer teaching and indirectly affected self-efficacy.

Das et. al. (1998) attempted to study the effect of intervention training while integrating it with teaching competence of student teachers.

The sample of 144 student teachers ranging from 16 to 26 years of age from seven colleges of education was taken. The data was treated by mean, SD and 't' test.

The result showed that the intervention strategy was not found to be effective in improving the general competence of student teachers. The institutions, which used diode skill integration intervention, observed significant mean gains on the general teaching competence of the students.

Leou S. (1998) studied teaching competencies assessment approaches for Mathematics teachers.

The following were the main purposes of the study. 1. to construct a list of assessment items for mathematics teachers. 2. to establish assessment models for mathematics teachers and 3. to develop evaluation instruments for mathematics teachers. The Delphi method and classroom observation technique were applied in this study. The results of the study have the following advantages: the assessment approaches and the instrument can be applied not only to confer a certificate on a qualified mathematics teachers, and to give feedback to the educational courses for student teachers, but also to employ or dismiss teachers, to set guidelines for professional development, and to establish criteria for the assessment of instructional competencies.

Verma (1998) tried to see the effect of microteaching skills on developing teaching competence among student teachers of science group.

The sample comprised 100 student teachers studying in six training colleges. The tools used included Ahluwalia's Teacher Attitude Inventory, Teaching Competency Assessment Scale, Observation Sheet, Assessment Guide and Microteaching Lesson-plan. The data were treated by using Mean, SD, ANOVA and graphical representation.

The study revealed that the experimental group showed better competencies in skills like skill of probing, questioning, reinforcement etc. The teaching competency of the female student teachers of science group was better in comparison to the male student and teachers of science using micro teaching approach. The teaching competency of urban student teachers was found to be better than that of their counterparts from rural areas. The teaching competency of the student teachers having no experience was better than that of those having experience.

Springer (2000) conducted a study of pre-service teachers incorporating technology into lessons during their practice - teaching experiences. Finding the right formula to incorporate coursework, field experiences, technology and assessment so that a level of competency achieve has been at the centre of debates and researches of teacher preparation programs. The researcher felt that very little has been done to determine the effectiveness of the technology aspect of practice teaching experience.

Pre- service teachers involved in their practice teaching experiences at three levels – elementary, middle and high school, were studied. Of particular interest were their experiences of incorporating technology into the lessons taught in the practice teaching setting. Data was collected through observations, interviews and the review of related documents.

The pre-service teachers used instructional technology for personal enjoyment, student interest and teachers' preparation programs. Recommendations include teaching the use of technology, screening cooperating teachers for instructional technology competencies and modeling by university professors.

Hall (2001) determined perceptions of beginning elementary teacher and principals regarding the preparedness of beginning teachers as related to stated competencies which were: Classroom Discipline, Competency in Teaching Specific Subjects, Students Evaluation, Teaching Methods and Strategies, Human Relations Skills and Competency in Teaching Special Students.

Teachers and principals responded that beginning teachers were most prepared in the competencies of Teaching Specific subject and Teaching Methods and Strategies.

There were statistically significant differences in the mean responses of teachers and principals to four of the six competencies- Teaching Specific Subjects, Students Evaluation, Teaching Methods and Strategies, and Teaching Special Students.

Al-Mutawa, A (2002) Conducted Evaluation of EFL Primary School Teachers' Competencies in Kuwait. The study assesses the current state of competencies of EFL primary school teachers. It also compares external and self -evaluation of these competencies for the teacher. An evaluation format was administered to 100 government EFL primary school teachers. It consisted to 28 competencies divided into three components, namely language level, lesson planning and implementation. The results indicated that these competencies were normally distributed among the sample with slight tendency to being positive. Statistically significant differences were found between males and females on the one hand, and between Kuwaitis and non- Kuwaitis on the other. There was also a wide discrepancy between the teachers' self – evaluation of competencies and the external evaluation in the three components. EFLPS teachers tend to overestimate their capabilities. Other variables such as teaching load, classroom density and teacher qualification proved non-significant. The study concluded with a number of educational implications relating to the results.

Farah (2002) studied on the topic A Comparative study of teaching competencies of the teachers trained through the formal system of education and those through the distance education system. The sample of the study consisted of 70 teachers trained through the formal system and 70 teachers trained through distance system. Students taught by these teachers were also randomly selected in order to administer the pupil liking scale and constituted the student sample. The findings indicate that – 1. There is no significant relationship between the knowledge and the attitude of teachers trained through distance mode and those trained through the formal mode. 2. A significant relationship between between the attitudes and skills of teachers. 3. A significant relationship between the attitudes of teachers and pupil liking. 4. No significant relationship between knowledge of teacher and pupil liking.

Saeed M. and Mahmood K. (2002) studied assessing competency of Pakistani primary school teachers in Mathematics, Science and pedagogy.

The study is aimed at investigating the competency level of primary school teachers in the disciplines of science, mathematics and pedagogy. The sample comprised 1800 randomly drawn primary teaching certificate (PMC) teachers working in different state primary and middle/elementary schools of 22 districts of the Punjab province. The competency was determined by developing standardized achievement tests in each of the three subjects. The results show teachers have a low level of competency in all these three areas. On average, their achievement rate remained 30.8 percent in mathematics, 34.1 percent in science and 39.2 percent in pedagogy, even below the minimum set criterion of 40 percent against each subject. Gender was found to be a significant indicator in the study that the competency level of female PTC teachers was lower than their male counterparts.

Bajwa Sukhwant (2003) tried to find effectiveness of competency-based teacher training strategy.

The present study is conducted to assess the effectiveness of competency based teacher training strategy in terms of i) development of general teaching competence of pre-service teachers. ii) change of attitude towards teaching of pre-service teachers. An intact sample of sixty teacher trainees from B.Ed. class was taken. Pre-test, post-test control group design was used. The sample was randomly divided into two groups. One of the two groups was randomly assigned as experiment group and other as control group. Experiment group was given training through competency-based teacher training strategy and control group through traditional teacher training approach. T-test was used to analyse the data. It was found that competency-based teacher training strategy was more effective than traditional teacher training strategy in developing general teacher competence. Neither the competency-based teacher training strategy nor the training model changed attitude of pupil-teachers towards teaching.

Smart, Roma (2003) attempted to Study the Professional Commitment of Primary School Teachers in Relation to Working Condition and Selected Personal Factors. The objectives of the study were: (i) to investigate the relationship between working conditions selected personal factors and professional commitment of primary school teachers (ii) to investigate the relationship between predictor variable such as working conditions and selected personal factors and the criterion variable (iii) to determine the relative contribution of the predictor variables i.e. working conditions and selected personal factors in predicting professional commitment of primary school teachers.

The sample comprised of 300 primary school teachers selected from government, private aided and private unaided schools of Lucknow city. A self-made tool on professional commitment of teachers was constructed and standardized by the researcher herself. To measure working conditions of primary school teachers was measured by self-developed possessing questionnaire with 40 items. Correlations and multiple regressions were used.

The findings depicted that (i) there exists a significant positive relationship between professional commitments and working conditions revealing that good working conditions of the schools will facilitate professional commitment of primary school teachers (ii) significant relationship is found between professional commitment and qualification, showing that teachers of lower qualifications are more committed than the highly qualified ones.

Natarajan P and Natesan N (2004) conducted a study to examine the effect of competency based teaching of environmental science through video on students' attainment at primary level.

Objectives of the study were (i) to study the effectiveness of competency based teaching of environmental science through video cassettes at V standard. (ii) to find out whether there is any significant difference between the mean scores of experimental group in the post-test. (iii) to find out whether there is any significant difference between the gap closure in control and experimental groups. Eighty six students studying in V standard drawn by purposive sampling technique from government aided school in Pudukkottai were the sample for this study. The findings of the study suggest that: Attainment of the concept and mastery of competencies can be possible through video cassette techniques at primary level. Competency based performance tests provide maximum exposure to children and motivate them to concentrate on the required competencies which help them to reach the mastery level. This competency based teaching of environmental science through video cassette method, helps in the acquisition of different performance skills and enhances the level of listening and reading abilities among the students. This method creates interest, attention and learning attitude among students.

Anandan K. and Rajasekaram P. (2005) studied on relationship between teaching competency and attitude towards teaching social science among distance learners of B.Ed.

The objectives of the study were to measure the relationship between teaching competency and attitude towards teaching social science with respect to sex, qualifications's and years of experience. The investigators selected 200 B.Ed. distance learners who selected social science as their methodology course in Madurai Kamaraj University. Two kinds of tools, namely, Teaching Competency Scale (TCS) and Attitude Towards Teaching Social Science (ATTSS) were developed and administered by the investigators. The collected data were processed by applying suitable statistical techniques. 'r' value was calculated to find out the relationship between the B.Ed. student-teachers' TCS and ATTSS. The results found that the relationship between TCS and ATTSS was positive among women, Bachelors Degree-holders and Masters Degree-holders.

Viswanathappa G. (2005) examined attitude towards teaching and teaching competence.

The objectives of the study were – 1. to measure the attitude towards teaching and teaching competence of student teachers at secondary level. 2. to obtain the Ed CET ranks, age, f :hers' occupation and father's education of the student teachers. 3. to fit the regression equation of student teacher's competence on attitude, Ed CET rank, father's education, father's occupation and age. 4. to predict the degree of contribution of predictor variables on criterion variable. The sample size of the study was 200 student teachers. Two tools namely attitude towards teaching profession and teaching competence scale developed by B. N. Panda and S.C. Panda, and Viswanathappa and Venkataiah respectively were used. Conclusions obtained were as 1. Attitude of student teachers towards teaching as a predictor variable predicts their teaching competence in lesson planning, presentation, closure of lesson and evaluation with various degrees of contribution and is significant at 0.01 level. 2. Admission test rank, age, father's occupation and father's education of student teachers as predictor variables do not predict their teaching competence in lesson planning, presentation, closure of lesson and evaluation. Even though there is a degree of contribution of these variables, this is not significant at 0.01 levels.

Raju B. and Viswanathappa A. (2007) conducted a study to find out competency of D.Ed. and B.Ed. trained teachers working in primary schools of Andhra Pradesh.

Main objectives of the study were – 1. to measure the teaching competency of B.Ed. and D.Ed., trained teachers working at primary level. 2. to compare the competency of D.Ed. and B.Ed., trained teachers in effectiveness of teaching. 3. to study the effectiveness of gender, locality, experience, qualification on teaching competence. For this study, 40 primary teachers, D.Ed. and B.Ed. trained teachers were selected from 20 schools of Nalgonda district in Andhra Pradesh. Two tools namely Teaching Competency Scale and Teacher Profile developed by the investigator were used. The findings of the study revealed the following. 1. There is no significant difference in teacher competency such as cognitive-based, performance-based, affective-based and consequence-based competency between rural and urban primary teachers. 2. There is no significant difference in teacher competency such as cognitive-based, performance-based, affective-based and consequence-based competency between gender (male/female), age, type of school and experience. 3. There is significant difference in teacher competency such as cognitive-based, performance-based, affective-based and consequence-based competency between D.Ed., and B.Ed., trained teachers working at primary level.

Shanbhag Shailaja P. (2007) conducted a study on effectiveness of a mastery learning instructional strategy in attainment of competencies in Mathematics.

Objectives of the study were – to develop a mastery learning instructional strategy (MILS) based on concrete to abstract learning continuum for the attainment of competencies in Mathematics. 2. to validate the instructional strategy in terms of content accuracy and organization : and language comprehensibility. 3. to study the effectiveness of the instructional stragey in terms of mastery of competencies in Mathematics and learners' liking towards mathematics. The sample of the study consisted of a total of 129 students of standard II from two schools: one experimental and one conventional. A criterion referenced achievement test was developed to measure the pre-requisite competencies of the students in Mathematics. The pre-test-post-test matched group design was employed in this study. Findings of the study indicate that all the pupils taught through the MLIS mastered all competencies in mathematics. Pupils taught through MLIS develop high liking towards Mathematics as it provides opportunities to play and perform activities as well as the success experiences that they get while learning.

Acar, Filiz Evran (2008) studied an Assessment of Social Studies Competency of Turkish Classroom Teachers. The aim of this study is to determine the importance of the competence and competence acquiring levels in the subject matter and subject teaching of the teachers who are graduated from the primary school teaching programmes of the educational faculties, towards the social studies. 270 teachers in total have been taken into the sampling group. The subject matter and subject teaching competencies of the classroom teachers for the social studies are determined with the analyze method. The questionnaire forms are prepared upon the determined competencies. Some meaningful differences between the averages of the social studies importance and acquiring levels were found. The teachers could not have the competency on the social studies in a manner compatible with its importance.

Singh, Seema (2008) conducted a study of teaching competency of secondary school teachers in relation to gender and teaching experience.

Main objectives of the study were – 1. to find out the difference in the level of teaching competency of male and female secondary school teachers. 2. to find out the difference in the level of teaching competency of teachers having teaching experience of less than 5 years and 6 to 10 years. 3 to find out the difference in the level of teaching competency of teachers having experience of less than 5 years and 11 to 20 years. 4. to find out the difference in the level of teaching competency of teachers having experience of less than 5 years and above 20 years. 5. to find out the difference in the level of teaching competency of teachers having experience of 6 to 10 years and 11 to 20 years. 6. to find out the difference in the level of teaching competency of teachers having experience of 6 to 10 years and above 20 years. 7. to find out the difference in the level of teaching competency of teachers having experience of 11 to 20 years and above 20 years. Sample of present study consists of ninety six secondary school teachers working in aided and private schools, chosen by systematic random method from 12 secondary schools of Lucknow. General teaching competency scale developed by Passi and Lalitha (1994) and self made personal data sheet were used. Findings of the study were as below – 1. The difference between teaching competency of male and female secondary school teachers was found non-significant. 2. The difference between teaching competency of teachers having teaching experience of less than five years and six to ten years; less than five years and eleven to twenty years; less than five years and above twenty years was found significant. 3. The difference between teaching competency of teachers having teaching experience of six to ten years and eleven to twenty years; six to ten years and above twenty years; eleven to twenty years and above twenty years was found non-significant.

Overview

From the review of related literature, cited above, it is clear that the findings related to the variables – Gender, Academic Qualification, Habitat, Training and Academic Qualification towards Teaching Competency, are neither consistent nor conclusive. In the opinion of the researcher, it is because of the use of diverse tools and techniques in the above research studies.

The purpose of present study is different from the earlier studies. The present study seeks to relate the teaching competencies with six important variables namely, gender, academic qualification, habitat, professional training, teaching experience and academic stream. It is hoped that this study would yield useful information relating to teaching competency of primary school teachers. The findings may also prove to be helpful in improving primary school practices in Uttar Pradesh.

3

Design and Procedure of the Study

3.1 INTRODUCTION

"A research design refers basically to the conceptual structure within which the research is conducted. It implies a plan to render the enquiry efficient so as to yield the truest possible generalizations, descriptions and predictions." – Pandey, K.P. (2005).

For the construction of a good research it is essential to prepare its appropriate design. In Kerlinger's (2007) opinion "Research design is the plan, structure and strategy of investigation conceived so as to obtain answers to research questions or programmes of the research. It includes an outline of what the investigator will do – from writing the hypothesis and their operational implication to the final analysis of the data."

The present chapter deals with the research methodology used in the present study. It discusses the method employed, the construction of self made tool, the sample chosen, collection of the data, and the techniques used for the statistical analysis.

3.2 METHOD

In the planning procedure a researcher has to decide on employing a suitable method. In fact, it is the most crucial decision on which depends the success of any research.

According to J.W. Best (2008), there are three types of researches – Historical research, Descriptive research and Experimental research, which describe what was, what is and what will be respectively. No one research method can be called superior or better than another because each method has its own qualities and limitations. It depends upon the problem and the researcher that which method is employed. Choice of the research method is determined by the nature of the problem.

Keeping in mind, the nature of the present research problem, Descriptive Survey method was found to be the most suitable for this study and hence it has been employed in this study. Descriptive method tells about what exists at present by determining the nature and degree of existing conditions. Because of the method's apparent ease and directness, descriptive method has undoubtedly been the most popular and most widely used research method in Education. According to Carter V. Good (2008) "In descriptive survey method the study of present situation or facts or incidents related with nature of a group of persons is done using techniques like induction, deduction, analysis, classification, measurement etc."

Many technical words like descriptive survey, normative survey, status survey and trend survey etc. are used for descriptive studies. If evidence of data concerning existing status is to be collected it is called status survey. If norms are to be decided from the available data for a specific group it is called normative survey. The work comparative is also a part of descriptive survey because the description of given data of survey is done by comparison among themselves and comparison of existing status with the established status and standards or with other researches.

In Descriptive Survey method, data collection is done from a large group. But if the group is very large and it is difficult to collect data and analyse the findings in such a large group, sample representative of the whole population is selected.

3.3 POPULATION

The well-specified and identifiable group is known as population or universe and the selected number of persons or objects is known as a sample. The generalized conclusions are technically known as the statistical inferences. A population, therefore, may be defined as any identifiable and well-specified group of individuals. All primary school teachers, all college teachers, all university students, all housewives etc, are examples of population. A population may be finite or infinite – a finite population is one where all the members can be easily counted; an infinite population is one whose size is unlimited and therefore, its members can not be counted. The population of university teachers is an example of finite population and the population of fishes in a river is an example of infinite population because the former can be counted whereas the latter can not be counted.

Likewise, a population may be real or imaginative – a real population is one which actually exists and an imaginative population is one which exists only in the imagination. In psychological and educational research on many occasions the population is imaginative. A measure based upon the entire population is called a parameter.

For this study the population constituted of the primary school teachers of Lucknow District.In the present investigation an attempt has been made to assess the teaching competencies of primary school teachers in Lucknow district in relation to Gender, Academic Qualification, Habitat, etc.

3.4 SAMPLE

A sample is a small proportion of the population that is selected for observation and analysis. By observing the characteristics of the sample, one can make certain inferences about the characteristics of the population from which it was drawn. One can also infer changes observed in the sample to changes that would likely have occurred in the population.

Sampling is essential for all research work, as one can not take the entire population since it consumes much time, energy and adds to difficulties and costs. Sampling is a technique of selecting a significant small group from a population which includes all the essential elements needed for investigation in hand. A sample would be representative of the whole universe. A sample can yield reliable results only if it is a true representative of the entire population which is unbiased and is of an adequate size.

To collect the requisite data for any research problem, the researcher has to sample the population concerned, since it is not possible to encompass the entire population. Some populations are so large that their study would be expensive in terms of time, money, effort and manpower.

Sampling is the process by which a relatively small number of individuals, objects or events is selected and analyzed in order to find out something about the entire population, from which it was selected. It helps to reduce expenditure, save time and energy, permit measurement of greater scope or produce greater precision and accuracy. Sampling procedure provide generalization on the basis of a relatively small proportion of the population. According to John. W. Best (2008) – "A sample is a small portion of population selected for analysis." In descriptive survey method it is very essential to select sample. Whether the sample truly represents the whole population depends upon the method of selection of sample and its size.

Various techniques have been derived for selecting a sample. Some of these are: – Simple Random Sampling, Stratified Sampling, Purposive Sampling, Cluster Sampling, Quota Sampling etc. In random sampling every member of the population has probability of coming into the sample, whereas in purposive sampling, the selection of sample depends on the basis of researcher's decision. The random sampling method is more scientific whereas the purposive sample is mostly more practical and useful.

In the present study researcher has used stratified random sampling method for selection of sample.

3.5 PROCEDURE OF SAMPLING IN THE PRESENT STUDY

In this study the researcher wanted to see the teaching competencies of primary school teachers in terms of Gender, Academic Qualification, Professional Training, Academic Stream, Habitat and Teaching Experience. The population of the study consisted of primary school teachers of Lucknow district. The researcher could not survey or investigate the entire population of teachers as it would entail a very lengthy process. Therefore the investigator decided to take a sample in order to make the job of data collection easier and less time taking. The list of recognized schools was acquired from the office of SCERT, Lucknow. After observing the list it was found that whole district is divided into 8 blocks/BRCs namely, Bakshi Ka Talab, Chinhat, Goshai Ganj, Kakori, Mall, Malihabad, Mohanlalganj and Sarojani Nagar of rural areas and 2 BRCs namely, Sahadatganj and Valdi Ka Khera of urban areas. Now 2 blocks/brcs i.e. Mall and Bakshi Ka Talab of rural areas were randomly selected. From the urban area both the BRCs were taken. Details are listed in Table No. 3.1. Teachers from the sample schools were randomly selected for the study.

3.6 NATURE AND SIZE OF THE SAMPLE

Table 3.1 shows the number of teachers included in the study under various categories. Out of the total sample of 200 teachers, equal numbers of teachers are drawn from rural and urban areas. On the whole, the sample includes 106 female and 94 male teachers.

Table 3.1. Total sample of Teachers (N=200)

Rural Schools		*Urban Schools*	
Mall N=50	Bakshi Ka Talab N=50	Sahadatganj N=50	Valdi Ka Khera N=50

3.7 VARIABLES OF THE STUDY

In educational researches variables are the conditions or characteristics that the researcher manipulates, controls or observes.

A research question aims to ask about the relationship between two or more variables. In order to state the expected answer to the research question, a research hypothesis is formulated which determines the expected relationship between the dependent and independent variables. In the present study there is one dependent variable and 6 independent variables.

3.7.1 Dependent Variable

"The Dependent variables are the conditions or characteristics that appear, disappear or change as the experimenter introduces, removes, or changes independent variables" (Best, 2008, p. 168). They are called dependent because they depend on the other variables. The dependent variable may be a test score, the number of errors, or measured speed in performing a task. Thus, the dependent variables are the measured changes in pupil performance attributable to the influence of the independent variables.

In the present study Teaching Competency is dependent variable as the effect of other variables has to be seen on it.

3.7.2 Independent Variable

"The independent variables are the conditions or characteristics that the experimenter manipulates in his attempt to ascertain their relationship to observed phenomena" (Ibid, p. 168).

Gender, Academic Qualification, Professional Training, Teaching Experience, Academic Stream and Habitat are independent variables in the present study, as these have been used to make the required predictions and to draw conclusions.

3.8 DATA COLLECTION DEVICES

After a brief discussion of sample and sampling process and variables to be treated in the present investigation, empirical tools to collect the responses on various dependent and independent variables also need to be described.

To collect the data for the study of any problem one may use various devices. For each and every type of research we need certain instruments to gather new facts or to explore new fields. The instruments thus employed as means are called 'Tools'.

Best John W. (2008) observes – "Like the tools in the Carpenter's box, each research tool is appropriate in a given situation to accomplish a particular purpose. Each data gathering device has both merits and hazards or delimitations."

In the Survey method of research, main tools used for data collection are – Test, Observation Schedule, Interview, Check list, Rating Scale and Score Card etc. The researcher has to select from the available tools, which will provide the data he required for the testing of hypothesis. In some situations, researcher may find that the existing research tools do not suit his purpose and so he may have to modify them or construct his own. It depends upon the researcher whether he uses standardized test available in his area or develop a tool by himself keeping in view the problem. Sometimes researcher can modify the standardized tool according to his need and use it accordingly. For purpose of research, standardized tools are the most commonly used ones, because they are considered more objectives, reliable and valid than the non-standardized ones. A standardized test is one that has specific directions for administration and scoring, a fixed set of test items, and has been administered to representative samples taken from the population for whom the test is intended, for the purpose of establishing norms. They make it possible to compare an individual's performance with other individuals belonging to his age or grade level. Thus the chief value of standardized tests for research purpose lies in their use as tools of comparison.

To measure the competencies of primary school teachers, different types of tools are available. Out of these, work done by Bruce W. Tuckmann (1975) and General Teaching Competency Scale of Passi and Lalitha (1994) are quite significant. The tool of Passi and Lalitha simply measures the general teaching competencies while the work of Tuckman is based on organized behaviour, dynamism, flexibility warmth, acceptance and creativity in western conditions. The readymade tools related to this area were not found suitable as they do not respond to the spirit of this study.

Thus, investigator developed a fresh tool to measure teaching competency of primary school teachers.

3.9 DEVELOPMENT OF TEACHING COMPETENCY TEST FOR PRIMARY SCHOOL TEACHERS

For the present study, the researcher developed "Teaching Competency Test for Primary School Teachers" himself.

3.9.1 Steps of Preparation of Tool

In developing the tool the investigator followed the steps mentioned as under :

1. Planning and writing the dimensions of the test.
2. Selection of the content from the different sources for the preparation of the test.
3. Preparation of the preliminary draft.
4. Collection of the opinion of the experts in the field.
5. Pre-testing of the preliminary draft.
6. Try out of the test for the item analysis.
7. Analysis of the results of the tryout / Item Analysis.
8. Final draft of the test.

Now the detailed description of the steps followed in construction of test is presented :

3.9.1.1 Planning and Writing the Dimensions of the Test

There are several conditions which determine the foundation and feasibility of test. Since no test was available to measure the teaching competencies the researcher wanted to study hence this tool was designed by the investigator. First of all, after study of different types of teaching competencies in the research literature, 5 major teaching competencies were selected for the present study. These are : (1) Contextual Competency, (2) Competencies related to other Educational Activities, (3) Content Competencies (4) Transactional Competencies and (5) Competencies to develop teaching learning material.

3.9.1.2 Selection of the Content from the Different Sources

The chief source of gathering information about the items related to different teaching competencies was the literature available in primary school books and other documents also.

This included setting up the objectives of the test and analysis of the source material pertaining to it. The first step towards it was to understand the nature of teaching competency and determine its dimensions. After browsing and scanning a lot of literature on teaching competencies and also after discussing with the field experts, following 5 teaching competency areas as mentioned above were decided to be included in this study.

3.9.1.3 Preparation of the Preliminary Draft

After identification of dimension, different type of items i.e. multiple choice, matching, filling the blanks, diagrammatic and open ended items were prepared for each dimension. Each item has been constructed with great care. Special attention has been given to the incorrect options. In the first draft of the scale 22 items for contextual competency, 28 items for other educational activities competency, 76 items for content competency, 52 items for transactional competency and 22 items for developing teaching learning material competency to each of the above mentioned dimension were framed. Following precautions were taken during development of items:

- Avoid statements that are irrelevant to the particular area.
- Avoid statements that are factual or capable of being interpreted as factual.
- Avoid statements that refer to the past rather than to the present.
- Avoid statements that may be interpreted in more than one way.
- Avoid the use of double negatives.
- Avoid the use of words that may not be understood by those who are to be given the completed scale.

- Whenever possible, statements should be in the form of simple sentences rather than in the form of compound or complex sentences.
- Words such as only, just, merely and others of a similar nature should be used with care and moderation in writing statements.
- Statements containing universals such as all, always, none and never often introduce ambiguity and should be avoided.
- Avoid statements that are likely to be endorsed by almost everyone or by almost no one.
- Select statements that are believed to cover the entire range of the affective scale of interest.
- Keep the language of the statements simple, clear and direct.
- Statements should be short, rarely exceeding twenty words.
- Each statement should contain only one complete thought.
- The statements framed were not too long because the excessive length introduces the irrelevant factor.
- The word used in the statements had only one meaning, so the confusion about the content may not exist.
- In one statement only one idea was presented.
- The number of statements in the initial format of the test was 100% more approximately than in the final draft.

In all 100 statements/items were framed covering all the dimensions of teaching competencies of primary school teachers.

3.9.1.4 Collection of the Opinion of Experts

The opinion of the experts from the field of teacher education, regarding the validity and weightage of these dimensions to assess the teaching competencies of primary school teachers was sought. Suggestions regarding content coverage, language and nature of the items were also gathered from them. Finally, investigator also consulted his supervisor to modify, include or exclude any item, if necessary. On the basis of expert opinion of the judges and the supervisor, the investigator made needful changes in the Test. Finally 100 items were finalized for the tool.

3.9.1.5 Pre-testing of the Preliminary Draft

The retained dimension-wise items were reshuffled from the view-point of the content. The scale so prepared was administered to 20 primary school teachers to see whether they felt any problem in the test. Their opinion about the content and the items was sought after they completed the test. This helped the researcher to discover whether the language of the test was ambiguous to the respondents and whether they understood and followed instructions clearly. Changes in the instructions, language and content were made after considering the reactions and comments of these teachers.

3.9.1.6 Try out of the Test

Instructions for administration and scoring procedure were finalized and the test was ready for tryout. For tryout the test was administered on a group of 25 primary school teachers who were asked to respond to each item in terms of their own agreement or disagreement with the statement. The administration procedure of the test was not a difficult one. The instructions given on the front page were self explanatory and needed no further guidance.

First of all the teachers were expected to fill up the personal data bank. For each group of items there was different type of responses. Instructions for each type of questions were clearly mentioned. There was no time limit for filling the test. The respondents were permitted to return it as soon as they completed it.

The items were then scored as per scoring process. Details of scoring are given further.

3.9.1.7 Item Analysis

Item analysis is the procedure by which an attempt is made to know how effectively a test item functions within the whole test. The item analysis could be done in two ways i.e. qualitative and quantitative. The investigator first did the qualitative analysis by changing the language of the items according to the opinion of the expert and the reactions of the sample chosen for the pre-test. Quantitative analysis includes the measurement of item difficulty and item discrimination. How hard is the item for the group tested and how well does it distinguished between the more able and less able students? These two aspects of an item are nearly independent of each other. The expectations being that very easy or very hard item can not discriminate well, if all testees mark the items correctly.

1. **A measure of discrimination** – After the test has been administered, score the answer sheets with the total score and then arrange all the scores in the ascending order beginning on top with smallest number and gaining down to the largest total score. Then divide the score into three groups – the highest 27% scores, the lowest 27% scores leaving aside the middle scores. Since it is not used in the item analysis for each item, t value has been calculated. Those items with t - value significant at .05 level of significance were finally selected.

2. A measure of Difficulty Level – Arranged all the answered total scores in the ascending order and divide these score into three parts. The first part contain the highest 27% scores, the lowest 27% scores in second part and middle 46% scores in the third part. Then following formula used for calculating difficulty-value :

$$p = \frac{R_u + R_l}{N_u + N_l}$$

Where

p — Index of Difficulty

R_u — Number of examinees answering correctly in the upper group

R_l — Number of examinees answering correctly in the lower group

N_u — Number of examinees in upper group

N_l — Number of examinees in lower group

Finally those items were selected that p-value (difficulty value) ranges between 0.5 to 0.8.

3.9.1.8 Final Draft of the Test

The category wise items retained after the first try-out were reshuffled from the view point of content. Selected items constituted the final tool consisting of 100 items.. The final draft so prepared is given at appendix A.

Now the draft was ready for the final try out for establishing the reliability and validity of the test.

3.9.2 Reliability of the Test

Reliability is the minimum condition which the test constructor should get for the accuracy of the test. Reliability refers to the consistency of scores obtained by the same individual and it also contributes to validity.

There are several ways of computing the reliability. The investigator examined them to find out the reliability of the constructed test.

The first method is known as test-re-test reliability method. The investigator found this method very time consuming and inconvenient. It was also found difficult to motivate the subjects, to perform the same task again.

Another way of computing the reliability is alternate form method. But this method was not feasible for the reliability of the present test, because it was not possible for the investigator to construct a test equivalent to the already constructed test in the limited time at his disposal.

Third way for establishing the reliability is through a single administration of the test i.e. split half method. The investigator found this method the most suitable because it needs only a single administration of the test. This method also gives a measure of internal consistency of the test.

To split the test into the comparable halves the investigator found the odd even method suitable leaving all other methods aside. Because it ensures that approximately the same amount of the time was devoted to each half and the testing conditions were nearly constant for the two halves. The conditions either internal or external to the examinees were not fluctuating with alternative items.

The investigator computed the reliability according to different major groups of test. First of all in each category the two half scores were obtained for each subject and then the correlation was found.

There are many formulae for measuring the reliability but finally the investigator decided to use Pearson Product moment formula (Garret, 1962) to compute the correlation co-efficient for split half reliability. The reliability computed by this formula was found to be .78.

3.9.3 Validity of the Test

Validity of a test concerns to what extent the test measures what it proposes to measure? There are three types of validity agreed upon by a joint committee of American Psychological Association (1954), American psychological association (1955) and the National Council of Measurement (1966) and also stated in the standards for educational and psychological tests and manuals (1966) named content, criterion and construct. Different authors labeled these by different names. The tool was shown to different experts to check content validity and it was found that tool is valid.

Thus the developed test was standardized and ready for data collection.

3.9.4 Final Structure of the Test

The description of properly standardized tool used for this study is given under the following heading:

- Main body of the test
- Administration of the test
- The scoring procedure of the test

A. Main Body of the Test

The whole test was classified in five major groups i.e. I, II, III, IV and V.

B. Administration of the Test

The administration procedure of the test was not a difficult one. The instructions were given at the front page. The instructions were self-explanatory and hence needed no guidance.

First of all, teachers were expected to fill up the personal data blank. Then they were asked to record their responses against each item. The respondents were permitted to return it as soon as they completed it.

C. Scoring of Test

A key was developed for scoring purpose. The details are as below:

1. To score 14 items of Part I, 1,2,3,4 and 5 marks was given for completely disagree, disagree, indefinite,

agree and completely agree respectively. Hence minimum and maximum scores become 14 and 70 respectively.

2. 1 mark was given to each item of Part II of tool. Total score of this section becomes 11.
3. 1 mark was again given to each item of part III of tool. Total score of this section becomes 26.
4. In part III, there were few items with 2 or 4 sub-questions. For these types of items 1/2 mark was awarded on each sub question and finally score was rounded to whole numbers. Thus the total score of this part becomes 60.
5. In section IV, 3 marks was given to all 11 items and hence total score of section IV becomes 33.

Marks scored by test of each primary school teacher are given in appendix I. Therefore, total score of whole tool is found 200.

3.10 STATISTICAL ANALYSIS OF DATA

Mean and S.D. of scores were computed and t – test was employed for comparing various groups or finding out differences between various groups. S.P.S.S. was used for analysis of data and statistical technique.

3.10.1 S.P.S.S. Package

SPSS is a software package used for conducting statistical analyses, manipulating data, and generating tables and graphs that summarize data. Statistical analyses range from basic descriptive statistics, such as averages and frequencies, to advanced inferential statistics, such as regression models, analysis of variance, and factor analysis. SPSS also contains several tools for manipulating data, including functions for recoding data and computing new variables as well as merging and aggregating data sets. SPSS also has a number of ways to summarize and display data in the form of tables and graphs.

Statistical Highlights for SPSS Base

1. Linear Regression
2. Factor Analysis
3. Two Step Cluster Analysis
4. K-means cluster analysis
5. Hierarchical cluster analysis

SPSS Base Includes

Descriptive Statistics

- Cross tabulations
- Frequencies
- Descriptive
- Explore
- Descriptive Ratio Statistics

Bivariate Statistics

- Means
- t – tests
- ANOVA
- Correlation
  - ➢ Bivariate
  - ➢ Partial
  - ➢ Distances
- Non – parametric tests

Prediction for numerical outcomes

- Linear regression

Prediction for identifying groups

- Factor analysis
- Two Step cluster analysis
- K-means cluster analysis
- Hierarchical cluster analysis
- Discriminant

More statistics for more powerful data analysis

4

Results of the Study on Teaching Competency of Primary School Teachers

A systematic treatment of the data is required to reach sound conclusions and to achieve the objectives of the study. Analysis of the data progresses through the systematic steps of scoring, tabulation, testing of the hypotheses, using appropriate statistical techniques followed by discussion of the results.

The purpose of analyzing the data is to summarize the complete observations in such a systematic way that they yield answers to the posed research problem. Thus with a view to achieve the objectives of the present study and to reach conclusions, the data has been analysed, discussed and interpreted.

As it has already been stated in the first chapter, the present investigation is an honest effort to examine the teaching competency of primary school teachers. To put it more specifically, the study aimed to find out the Teaching Competencies of Primary School Teachers in relation to Gender, Academic Qualification, Habitat, etc.

In order to realize this aim the representative sample was drawn from the list of primary school teachers of Lucknow district.

In the present chapter an attempt has been made to analyze and interpret the data collected in the manner described in chapter III. As mentioned in chapter III, the data are collected in regard to five teaching competencies, namely educational activities competency, contextual competency, transactional competency, content competency and development of teaching learning material competency.

The presentation and discussion of results in this chapter follows according to the objectives of the study.

Critical ratio (CR) was computed for the purpose of testing the significance of difference between Means at .05 level. The technique was tested on overall teaching competency, comprising of five dimensions.

4.1 LEVEL OF TEACHING COMPETENCIES

The first objective was to find out the level of teaching competencies of Primary School Teachers working in Lucknow district. Relating to this objective the hypothesis framed by the researcher reads as under:

H_1: "Majority of Primary School Teachers will be found to possess 'high' / 'very high' level of Teaching Competency".

To meet the aforesaid objective and finally answer the concerned hypothesis, the scores obtained by teachers on each dimension of the teaching competency were divided into four levels, viz. very high, high, low and very low and, frequency and percentage of teachers falling under each level were computed. The results thus obtained are summarized in table 4.1. Figure 4.1 further depicts these results.

Table 4.1. Distribution of teachers at different levels of teaching competencies

SN	*Teaching Competency*	*Very High N*	*%*	*High N*	*%*	*Low N*	*%*	*Very Low N*	*%*
1.	Educational Activities	25	12.5	128	64	43	21.5	4	2
2.	Contextual	22	11	123	61.5	45	22.5	10	5
3.	Transactional	8	4	114	57	61	30.5	17	8.5
4.	Content	20	10	87	43.5	67	33.5	26	13
5.	Development of Teaching Learning Material	15	7.5	35	17.5	85	42.5	65	32.5
	Overall position	18	9	97.4	48.7	60.2	30.1	24.4	12.2

It is clear from table 4.1 that in the distribution of teachers for the teaching competency in educational activities the maximum number of teachers, i.e. 64 % belong to 'high' level, while 21.5 % to 'low' level, 12.5 % to 'very high' level and only 2 % to 'very low' level. In contextual

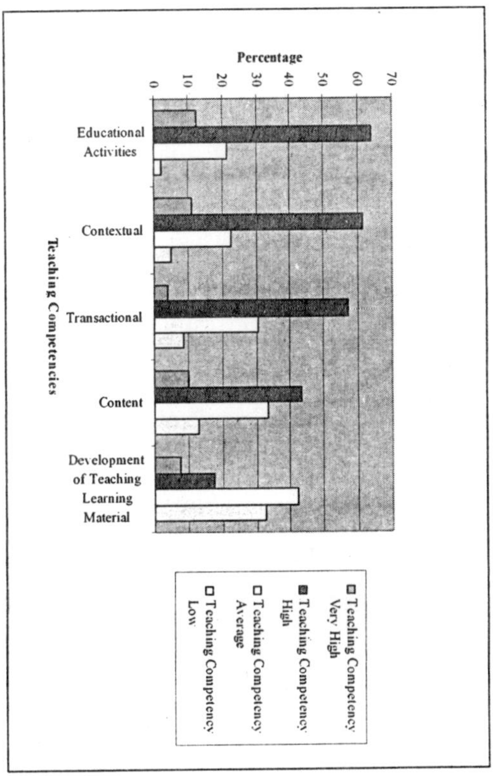

Fig. 4.1. Graphical Presentation of Teaching Competencies of Primary School Teachers

competency, 61.5% teachers are found at 'high' level, 22.5 % at 'low' level, 11 % at 'very high' level and 5 % at 'very low' level. For transactional competency this proportion is: 57 % at 'high' level, 30.5 % at 'low' level, 8.5 % at 'very low' level and only 4 % at 'very high' level. In content competency the proportion of teacher at 'high' level is 43.5 %, at 'low' level 33.5 %, at 'very low' level 13 % and at 'very high' level 10%. For development of teaching learning material competency, 42.5 % teachers are found at 'low' level, 32.5 % at 'very low' level, 17.5 % at 'high' and 7.5 % at 'very high' level.

Considered on the whole, the proportion of teachers with 'high' level of teaching competency is 48.7 %, with 'low' level 30.1 %, with 'very low' level 12 % and with 'very high' level 9 %. If the same results are seen in terms of number of teachers falling in different categories of teaching competency, the data reveal that approximately 115 out of 200 are observed to have either 'high' or 'very high' level of teaching competency (18 cases in 'high' and 97.4 cases in 'very high' category) while 85 out of 200 teachers are found to have either 'low' or 'very low' teaching competency (62.2 cases in 'low' and 24.4 cases in 'very low' category).

Thus to conclude, the hypothesis 1 of this study which anticipated that majority of teachers will be found to posses 'high' / 'very high' level of teaching competency is confirmed.

4.2 GENDER-WISE ANALYSIS OF TEACHING COMPETENCY

The second objective of this study necessitated a comparison between male and female teachers with respect to their Teaching Competency scores for the five dimensions of teaching competency namely, educational activities, contextual, transaction, content and development of teaching-learning material. The results of this comparison are presented in table 4.2 and figure 4.2.

Table 4.2. Gender -Wise Comparison of Teachers for their Teaching Competencies

Teaching Competencies	*Gender*	*N*	*Mean*	*Std. Deviation*	*Std. Error of Difference*	*t - Value*
Educational Activities	Male	94	47.67	8.69	1.19	.67
	Female	106	48.48	8.13		
Contextual	Male	94	7.02	2.29	.30	1.34
	Female	106	7.43	2.00		
Transactional	Male	94	13.90	4.40	.65	.07
	Female	106	13.95	4.79		
Content	Male	94	29.93	11.07	1.70	.50
	Female	106	30.78	13.01		
Development of Teaching Learning Material	Male	94	11.03	7.77	1.10	1.38
	Female	106	12.56	7.82		
Total Teaching Competency	Male	94	109.55	26.20	3.89	1.07
	Female	106	113.74	28.91		

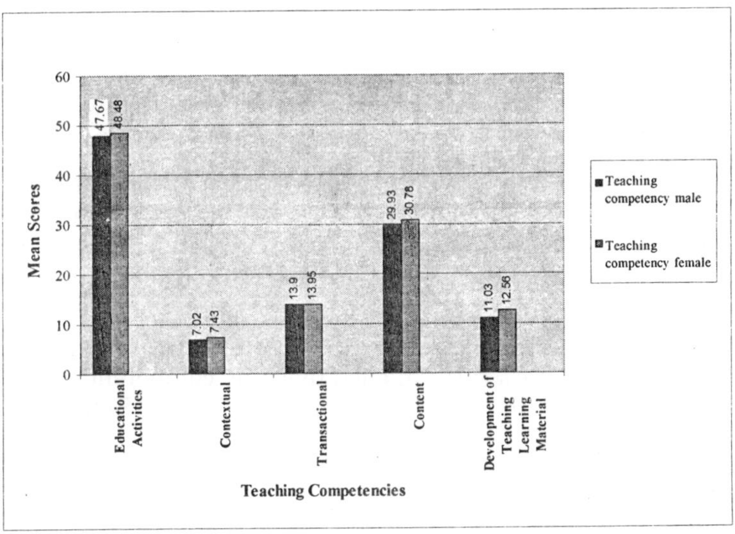

Fig. 4.2. Mean Scores on Teaching Competency obtained by Male and Female Teachers

Perusal of the table 4.2 indicates that for all dimensions of teaching competency namely, 'Educational Activities', 'Contextual', 'Transactional', 'Content', and 'Development of Teaching-Learning Material', no significant difference is found between the mean scores obtained by male and female teachers. Both the groups are observed equal on all dimensions. Also for total teaching competency the t-value for the two groups has not reached the .05 level of significance. This shows that gender of primary school teacher is not an important factor of teaching competency.

In conclusion, the hypothesis – 2 of this study that "There is no significant difference in mean scores of teaching competency of primary school teachers with respect to their gender" is retained.

4.3 ACADEMIC QUALIFICATION-WISE ANALYSIS OF TEACHING COMPETENCY

The third objective of the study led to a comparison of teaching competency of primary school teachers with respect to their academic qualification. In this regard the hypothesis formulated by the investigator is as below:

H_3 "There is no significant difference in the mean scores of teaching competency of primary school teachers with respect to their academic qualification."

To achieve the above mentioned objective and test the concerned hypothesis, the data were analyzed for each of the five teaching competencies separately. These five teaching competencies are educational activities competency, contextual competency, transactional competency, content competency and development of teaching learning material competency respectively. In each teaching competency, there were six comparison groups, namely, High School vs. Intermediate, High School vs. graduate, High School vs. Post Graduate, Intermediate vs. graduate, graduate vs. Post Graduate and Intermediate vs. Post Graduate. To compare these groups, Mean, S.D. and S.E. have been computed and t-test applied. Results of these analyses are summarized in tables 4.3 to 4.7 and also figures in 4.3 to 4.7.

4.3.1 Competency of Educational Activities

Table 4.3 and figure 4.3 present the summary of results of educational activities.

Table 4.3. Qualification-Wise Comparison of Teachers for their Teaching Competency (Educational Activities)

Teaching Competency	*Qualifications*	*N*	*Mean*	*Std. Deviation*	*Std. Error Difference*	*t-Value*
	High School	20	41.65	7.46	2.14	1.40
	Intermediate	47	44.66	8.27		
	High School	20	41.65	7.46	1.67	3.72**
	Graduate	82	47.88	6.52		
	High School	20	41.65	7.46	1.91	6.89**
Educational	Postgraduate	49	54.88	7.13		
Activities	Intermediate	47	44.66	8.27	1.40	2.28*
	Graduate	82	47.88	6.52		
	Graduate	82	47.88	6.52	1.24	5.60**
	Postgraduate	49	54.88	7.13		
	Intermediate	47	44.66	8.27	1.58	6.46**
	Postgraduate	49	54.88	7.13		

* = $p < 0.05$
* *= $p < 0.01$

It is clear from table 4.3 that mean and S.D. of teaching competency scores for teachers possessing high school qualification are 41.65 and 7.46 respectively and for those with intermediate qualification are 44.66 and 8.27 respectively. The t-value is 1.40 which is not significant at .05 level. This indicates that there is no significant difference in educational activities teaching competency between teachers possessing high school and intermediate qualifications.

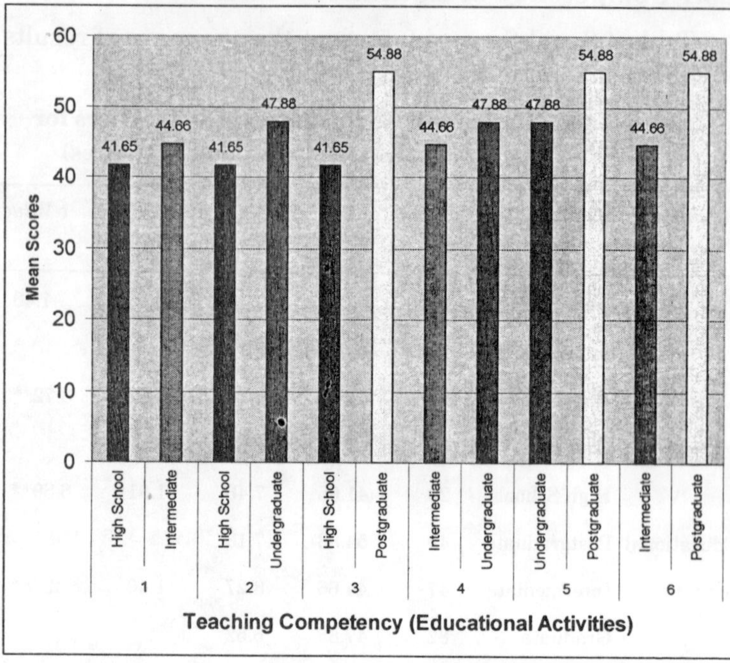

Fig. 4.3. Mean scores on 'Educational Activities' dimension of Teaching Competency obtained by teachers having different qualifications

The mean and S.D. of educational activity competency scores for teachers with high school qualification are 41.65 and 7.46 respectively and for those with graduate qualification are 47.88 and 6.52 respectively. Thus, the mean value of high school pass teachers is less in comparison of graduate teachers. The computed t-value is 3.72 which is significant at .01 level, which indicates that there is a significant difference between the teachers belonging to high school and graduate qualifications with regard to their competency in educational activities. On the basis of mean differences between the two groups it may be said that the teachers whose qualification is graduate are more competent in this competency in comparison to the teachers whose qualification is only high school.

Perusal of the table 4.3 makes it clear that mean and S.D. of high school pass teachers are 41.65 and 7.46 respectively and those of post graduate teachers are 54.88 and 7.13 respectively. The t-value is 6.89 which is significant at .01 level.

The t-value in case of intermediate and graduate teachers with regard to educational activities competency is 2.28, which is also significant at .05 level. Table 4.3 shows that mean and S.D. of scores of graduate teachers are 47.88 and 6.52 respectively whereas of post graduate teachers are 54.88 and 7.13 respectively. The t-value is 5.60 which is significant at .01 level. This shows that there is a significant difference in educational activities competency between teachers possessing graduate and post graduate qualifications.

Further, table 4.3 shows that mean and S.D. of scores of intermediate teachers are 44.66 and 8.27 respectively and of post graduate teachers it is 54.88 and 7.13 respectively. The t-value is 6.46 which is significant at .01 level. Since, mean score of post graduate teachers is more in comparison to intermediate teachers, hence, it is clear that post graduate teachers are more competent in comparison of intermediate teachers with regard to educational activities competency.

In conclusion, it is observed that out of six competencies of teaches possessing different qualifications namely, high school and intermediate, high school and graduate, high school and post graduate, intermediate and graduate, graduate and post graduate, intermediate and post graduate, in five comparisons namely, high school and graduate, high school and post graduate, intermediate and graduate, graduate and post graduate, intermediate and post graduate the mean differences are statistically significant. Only in one comparison namely, between high school and intermediate the mean difference is not significant with regard to educational activities teaching competency.

4.3.2 Contextual Competency

Table 4.4 and figure 4.4 present the summary of results in regard to Contextual dimension of Teaching Competency.

Table 4.4. Qualification-Wise Comparison of Teachers for Their Teaching Competency (Contextual)

Teaching Competency	*Qualifications*	*N*	*Mean*	*Std. Deviation*	*Std. Error Difference*	*t - Value*
	High School	20	5.75	2.48	.61	1.40
	Intermediate	47	6.62	2.24		
	High School	20	5.75	2.48	.51	3.48**
	Graduate	82	7.55	1.95		
	High School	20	5.75	2.48	.54	3.85**
Contextual	Postgraduate	49	7.84	1.83		
	Intermediate	47	6.62	2.24	.39	2.37*
	Graduate	82	7.55	1.95		
	Graduate	82	7.55	1.95	.33	.84
	Postgraduate	49	7.84	1.83		
	Intermediate	47	6.62	2.24	.41	2.91**
	Postgraduate	49	7.84	1.83		

* = $p < 0.05$

* *= $p < 0.01$

Perusal of the table 4.4 shows that out of six comparisons, in 4 comparisons the t-values have turned out to be statistically significant. These four comparisons are between teachers with high school and graduate qualification (t-value 3.48), between teachers having high school and post graduate qualification (t-value 3.85), between teachers possessing intermediate and graduate qualification (t value 2.37) and between teachers having intermediate and post graduate qualification (t-value 2.91). Teachers having high school qualification are observed to be almost equal (Mean 5.75) to those holding intermediate qualification (Mean 6.62). Similarly, graduate qualification holders are found to be at almost equal level (Mean 7.55) as compared to postgraduate qualification holders (Mean 7.84). No significant difference is observed in these two comparisons (i.e. between high school and intermediate and between graduate and post graduate).

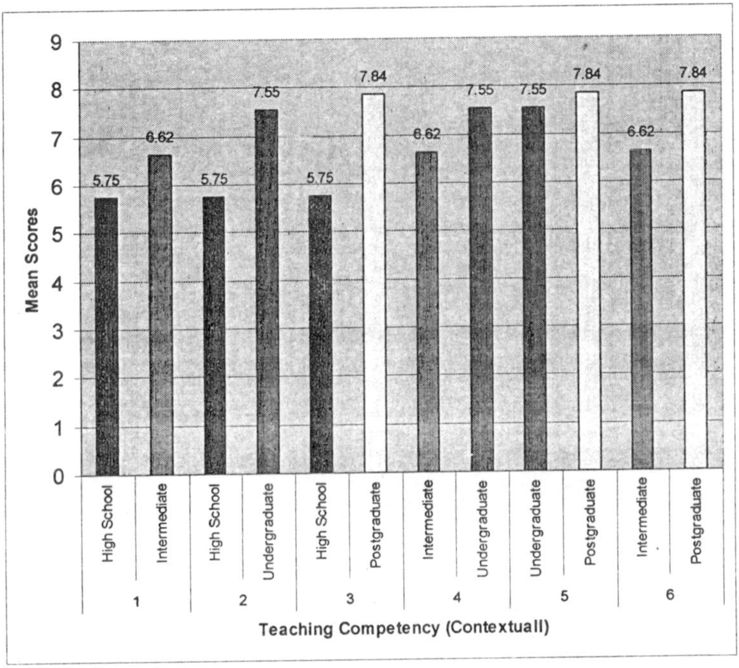

Fig. 4.4. Mean scores on 'Contextual' dimension of Teaching Competency obtained by teachers having different qualifications

Thus, the conclusion that flows from this analysis is that on contextual dimension of teaching competency primary school teachers having postgraduate qualification are observed to be significantly more competent than intermediate and high school qualification holders, while graduate teachers are found to be significantly more competent than intermediate and high school pass teachers.

4.3.3 Transactional Competency

Table 4.5 summarizes the data with regard to 'Transactional' dimension of teaching competency for the different qualification groups of teachers. Figure 4.5 further illustrates the position.

Table 4.5. Qualification-Wise Comparison of Teachers for their Teaching Competency (Transactional)

Teaching Competency	*Qualifications*	*N*	*Mean*	*Std Deviation*	*Std. Error Difference*	*t - Value*
	High School	20	10.65	4.33	1.17	1.74
	Intermediate	47	12.70	4.44		
	High School	20	10.65	4.33	1.12	2.88**
	Graduate	82	13.90	4.56		
	High School	20	10.65	4.33	1.01	5.79**
Transactional	Postgraduate	49	16.55	3.62		
	Intermediate	47	12.70	4.44	.82	1.46
	Graduate	82	13.90	4.56		
	Graduate	82	13.90	4.56	.72	3.66**
	Postgraduate	49	16.55	3.62		
	Intermediate	47	12.70	4.44	.82	4.64**
	Postgraduate	49	16.55	3.62		

* = $p < 0.05$

* *= $p < 0.01$

An observation of table 4.5 and figure 4.5 reveals that like preceding two analyses in the present analysis also the post graduate teachers have once again been observed to possess a higher level of teaching competency than their counterparts possessing other than postgraduate qualification. Mean score obtained by postgraduate teachers on 'transactional' dimension of teaching competency is 16.55 as compared to 13.90, 12.70 and 10.65 obtained by teachers having graduate, intermediate and high school qualification respectively.

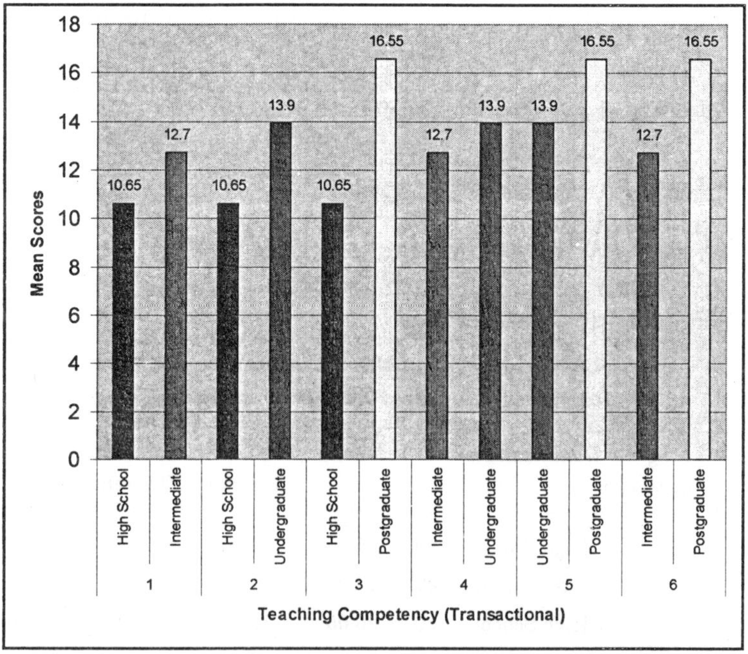

Fig. 4.5. Mean scores on 'Transactional' dimension of Teaching Competency obtained by teachers having different qualifications

To see the significance of difference between the various comparison groups, the table shows that out of the six comparisons, in four comparisons the mean differences are observed to be significant. These comparisons are (1) graduate vs. high school in which graduates have surpassed the high schools, (2) high school vs. post graduate in which post graduates have excelled the high schools, (3) graduate vs. post graduate in which post graduates have scored higher than graduates and (4) intermediate vs. post graduate in which again post graduates have scored higher than intermediates. In remaining comparisons the t-ratios are not found to be statistically significant.

Now, it may be concluded that the primary school teachers having post graduate qualification are better than their counterparts having graduate, intermediate and high school qualification on 'transactional' dimension of the teaching competency.

4.3.4 Content Competency

The next analysis is carried out for 'content' aspect of teaching competency. The relevant data in this regard are presented in table 4.6. Figure 4.6 is the graphical presentation of the mean scores obtained by the different comparison groups of teachers formed on the basis of their academic qualification.

Table 4.6. Qualification-Wise Comparison of Teachers for Their Teaching Competency (Content)

Teaching Competency	*Qualifications*	*N*	*Mean*	*Std. Deviation*	*Std. Error Difference*	*t - Value*
	High School	20	25.05	10.50	2.99	1.00
	Intermediate	47	28.06	11.48		
	High School	20	25.05	10.50	2.95	1.54
	Graduate	82	29.62	12.13		
	High School	20	25.05	10.50	3.04	3.52**
Content	Postgraduate	49	35.78	11.83		
	Intermediate	47	28.06	11.48	2.14	.72
	Graduate	82	29.62	12.13		
	Graduate	82	29.62	12.13	2.157	2.85**
	Postgraduate	49	35.78	11.83		
	Intermediate	47	28.06	11.48	2.38	3.24**
	Postgraduate	49	35.78	11.83		

* = $p < 0.05$

* *= $p < 0.01$

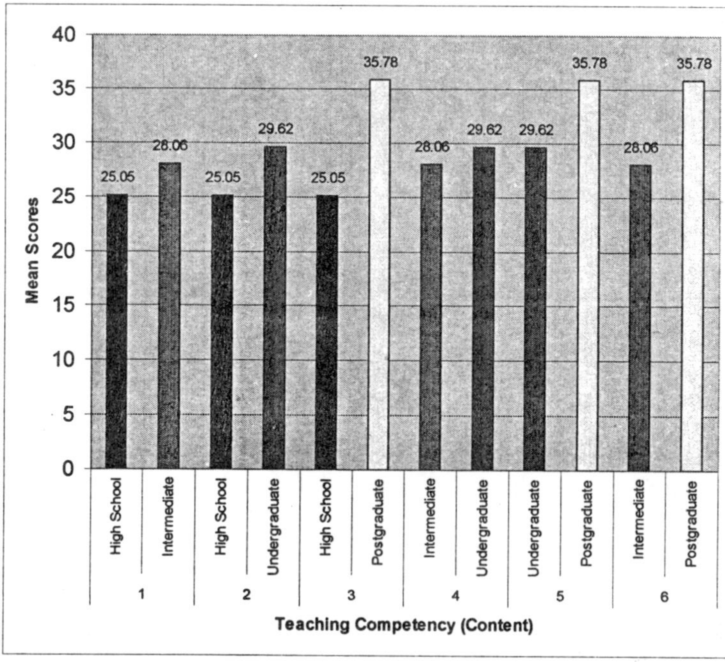

Figure 4.6. Mean scores on 'Content' dimension of Teaching Competency obtained by teachers having different qualifications

A look of table 4.6 reveals that out of the six comparisons made between teachers with different academic qualifications, in three comparisons namely high school and post graduate, graduate and post graduate, intermediate and post graduate, the difference between mean scores for 'content' dimension of teaching competency have turned out to be statistically significant. The computed t-ratios of above stated three groups for difference in means are 3.52, 2.85 and 3.24 respectively which are significant at .01 level. Like preceding analysis, in this analysis also, highly qualified teachers are observed to have higher teaching competency than less qualified teachers.

In other three comparison groups namely high school and intermediate, high school and graduate and intermediate and graduate, the t- values have not reached the level of significance. Therefore, it is concluded that the academic qualification has failed to show any impact on teaching competency of these groups but the mean scores of above groups indicate that better qualified teachers have better impact on the 'content' teaching competency of these groups.

4.3.5 Competency of 'Development of Teaching-Learning Material'

Table 4.7 summarizes the data with regard to 'Development of teaching –Learning Material' dimension of the teaching competency for the different qualification wise groups of teachers. Figure 4.7 further illustrates the position.

Table 4.7. Qualification-Wise Comparison of Teachers for their Teaching Competency (Development of Teaching-Learning Material)

Teaching Competency	*Qualifications*	*N*	*Mean*	*Std. Deviation*	*Std.Error Difference*	*t – Value*
	High School	20	8.05	4.78	1.81	2.14*
	Intermediate	47	11.96	7.49		
	High School	20	8.05	4.78	1.34	1.68
	Graduate	82	10.32	7.15		
	High School	20	8.05	4.78	2.10	3.67**
Development of Teaching Learning Material	Postgraduate	49	15.78	8.85		
	Intermediate	47	11.96	7.492	1.34	1.21
	Graduate	82	10.32	7.151		
	Graduate	82	10.32	7.15	1.49	3.66**
	Postgraduate	49	15.78	8.85		
	Intermediate	47	11.96	7.49	1.67	2.28*
	Postgraduate	49	15.78	8.85		

* = $p < 0.05$
* *= $p < 0.01$

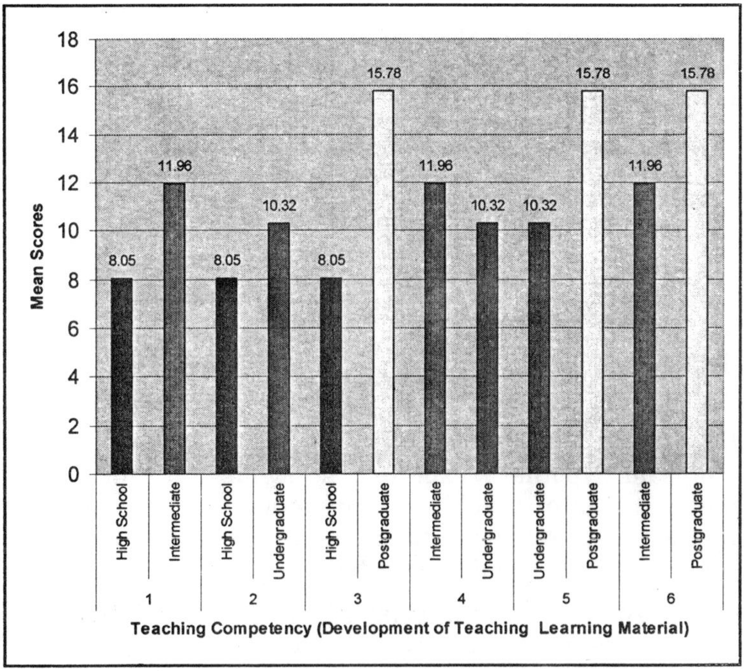

Fig. 4.7. Mean scores on 'Development of Teaching-Learning Material' dimension of Teaching Competency obtained by teachers having different qualifications

Perusal of table 4.7 and also figure 4.7 reveals that out of six comparisons, in four comparisons the t-values have turned out to be statistically significant. These four comparisons are between teachers with high school and intermediate qualification (t-value 2.14), between teachers having undergone graduate and post graduate qualification (t-value 3.67), between teachers possessing graduate and postgraduate qualification (t-value 3.66) and between teachers having intermediate and post graduate qualification (t-value 2.28). Teachers having graduate qualification are observed to be significantly higher (Mean 10.32) than those holding high school (Mean 8.05) qualification teachers having graduate qualification are observed to be significantly lower (Mean 10.32) than those holding intermediate (Mean 11.96) qualifications on 'development of teaching-learning material' dimension of the teaching competency.

Thus, the conclusion that flows from this analysis is that primary school teachers having post graduate qualification are observed to be more competent in comparison of graduate, intermediate and high school qualification teachers but it was also found that intermediate teachers are more competent in 'development of teaching-learning material' dimension of teaching competency than graduate degree holders.

Thus, to conclude on this section and decide upon the hypothesis – 3 of this study, it may be stated that the aforesaid hypothesis expected "no significant difference in mean scores of teaching competency of primary school teachers with respect to their academic qualification". This null hypothesis could be rejected as stated below:

1. In case of comparison between high school and intermediate qualification teachers, the null hypothesis was only rejected for 'development of teaching-learning material' dimension of the Teaching Competency Test. For this dimension the intermediate qualification teachers were observed to possess greater teaching competency than high school passed teachers.
2. In case of comparison between high school and graduate qualification teachers also the null hypothesis was rejected for 'Educational Activity', 'contextual' and 'transactional' dimensions of Teaching Competency. On these three dimensions the graduate teachers were found to possess greater teaching competency than teachers holding high school qualification. On other two dimensions of teaching competency namely, content and development of teaching-learning material, both the groups of teachers were found to be equal.
3. In case of comparison between groups of teachers holding high school and post graduate qualification,

the null hypothesis is rejected for all the dimensions of teaching competency. On all the five dimensions of Teaching Competency Test these two groups of teachers were found to possess unequal level of teaching competency.

4. In case of comparison between intermediate and graduate qualified teachers the null hypothesis was rejected for 'educational Activities' and 'Contextual' dimension of teaching competency. On these two dimensions of 'Teaching Competency Test, teachers having qualification graduation were found to be significantly more competent than teachers having qualification intermediate. On all other three dimensions the null hypothesis is accepted but it was observed that teachers having qualification intermediate have better teaching competency than graduate teachers for 'development of teaching-learning material' dimension of teaching competency.
5. In case of comparison between group of teachers holding qualification graduate and post graduate, the null hypothesis was rejected for 'Educational Activities', 'Transactional', 'Content' and 'Development of Teaching-Learning Material' dimension of teaching competency. On these dimensions of Teaching Competency Test, the post graduate teachers were found to be significantly more competent than teachers holding intermediate qualification. On remaining one dimension namely 'Contextual' dimension the null hypothesis is accepted.
6. In case of teachers between intermediate and post graduate qualification teachers the null hypothesis was rejected for all five dimensions of the teaching competency. On these dimensions of Teaching Competency Test post graduate teachers were observed to possess greater teaching competency than teachers holding qualification intermediate.

4.4 PROFESSIONAL TRAINING-WISE ANALYSIS OF TEACHING COMPETENCY

Objective 4 of the present study, namely, 'to compare the teaching competency of primary school teachers with respect to their training' required a comparison between teachers holding different professional qualifications such as JBT, BTC, VBTC and B.Ed. in terms of scores obtained by them on different dimensions of the competency test developed by the researcher for this study. Tables 4.8 to 4.12 contain the analysis of data in this regard and further these results are graphically shown in figures 4.8 to 4.12.

4.4.1 Competency of Educational Activities

Table 4.8 and also the figure with the same number adumbrates the summary of results relating to 'Educational Activities' dimension of Teaching Competency Test.

Table 4.8. Training-Wise Comparison of Teachers for their Teaching Competency (Educational Activities)

Teaching Competency	*Training*	*N*	*Mean*	*Std. Deviation*	*Std. Error Difference*	*t - Value*
	JBT	19	42.58	9.23	1.92	2.66*
	BTC	127	47.72	7.62		
	JBT	19	42.58	9.23	2.69	3.75**
	VBTC	50	51.56	8.73		
	JBT	19	42.58	9.23	4.89	.08
Educational	B.ED.	4	43.00	6.58		
Activities	BTC	127	47.72	7.62	1.40	2.72**
	VBTC	50	51.56	8.73		
	BTC	127	47.72	7.62	3.85	1.22
	B.ED.	4	43.00	6.58		
	VBTC	50	51.56	8.73	4.41	2.91*
	B.ED.	4	43.00	6.58		

* = $p < 0.05$

* *= $p < 0.01$

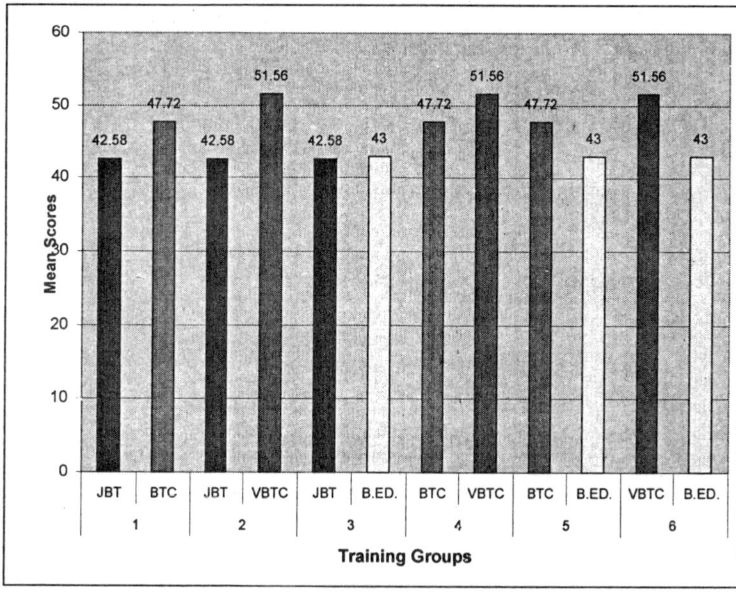

Fig. 4.8. Mean scores on 'Educational Activities' dimension of Teaching Competency obtained by different Training groups of teachers.

An inspection of table 4.8 indicates that out of six comparisons, in 4 comparisons the t-values have turned out to be statistically significant. These four comparisons are between teachers with JBT and BTC trainings (t-value 2.66), between teachers having undergone JBT and VBTC trainings (t-value 3.75), between teachers holding BTC and VBTC qualifications (t-value 2.72) and between teachers having VBTC and B.Ed. degrees respectively. Teachers having JBT qualification are observed to be significantly lower (Mean 42.58) than those holding BTC (Mean 47.72) or VBTC (Mean 51.56) qualifications on 'Educational Activities' dimension of the teaching competency. On the other hand, BTC qualification holders are found to be significantly lower (Mean 47.72) than VBTC qualification holders (Mean 51.56). In comparison between B.Ed. degree holders and VBTC teachers the latter have been observed to be significantly higher than the former (t-value 2.91) on the 'Educational Activities' dimension of Teaching Competency Test.

Thus, the conclusion that flows from this analysis is that primary school teachers having professional qualification of VBTC are observed to be more competent in 'educational activities' dimension of teaching competency, than JBT, BTC and B.Ed. degree holders.

4.4.2 Contextual Competency

The next analysis is in regard to contextual dimension of teaching competency. Here the comparison groups of teachers, formed on the basis of their professional qualifications, are compared with each other for scores obtained by them on the contextual dimension of the Teaching Competency Test developed and used by the investigator in this study.

Table 4.9 and also Figure 4.9 exhibits the results of the present analysis.

Table 4.9. Training-Wise Comparison of Teachers for their Teaching Competency (Contextual)

Teaching Competency	*Training*	*N*	*Mean*	*Std. Deviation*	*Std. Error Difference*	*t - Value*
	JBT	19	6.68	2.40	.55	.92
	BTC	127	7.20	2.24		
	JBT	19	6.68	2.40	.53	1.63
	VBTC	50	7.56	1.82		
	JBT	19	6.68	2.40	1.27	.44
	B.ED.	4	7.25	1.70		
Contextual	BTC	127	7.20	2.24	.32	1.11
	VBTC	50	7.56	1.82		
	BTC	127	7.20	2.24	1.13	.04
	B.ED.	4	7.25	1.70		
	VBTC	50	7.56	1.82	.94	.32
	B.ED.	4	7.25	1.70		

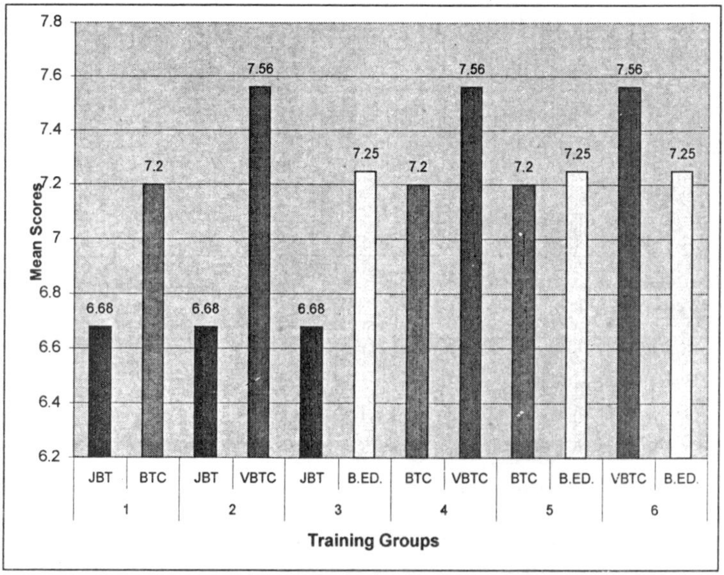

Fig. 4.9. Mean scores on 'Contextual' dimension of Teaching Competency obtained by different Training groups of teachers

It may be readily perceived from table 4.9 that none of the comparison groups differ from each other significantly in the matter of contextual dimension of teaching competency. They all appear to be almost equal in this respect. No impact of pre-service professional training obtained by them is seen to be statistically significant. However, if we look to the trend in the data, the table reveals that it is the group of VBTC teachers who have scored higher than all other comparison groups. It may be recalled here that in the preceding analysis also the VBTC teachers were observed to be more competent than teachers holding other professional qualifications.

However, since none of the t-values in this analysis have reached the level of statistical significance the null hypothesis is accepted in this case. It is concluded that professional training of teachers has failed to show any impact on the 'Contextual' teaching competency of these teachers.

4.4.3 Transactional Competency

Data pertaining to 'Transactional' dimension of the teaching competency are summarized in table 4.10 and graphically presented in figure 4.10.

Table 4.10. Training-Wise Comparison of Teachers for their Teaching Competency (Transactional)

Teaching Competency	*Training*	*N*	*Mean*	*Std. Deviation*	*Std. Error Difference*	*t - Value*
	JBT	19	11.53	4.12	1.11	2.23*
	BTC	127	14.02	4.57		
	JBT	19	11.53	4.12	1.14	3.06**
	VBTC	50	15.02	4.27		
	JBT	19	11.53	4.12	2.43	1.03
Transactional	B.ED.	4	9.00	5.88		
	BTC	127	14.02	4.57	.72	1.37
	VBTC	50	15.02	4.27		
	BTC	127	14.02	4.57	2.34	2.14
	B.ED.	4	9.00	5.88		
	VBTC	50	15.02	4.27	2.27	2.64*
	B.ED.	4	9.00	5.88		

* = $p < 0.05$,
* *= $p < 0.01$

A look at table 4.10 and also figure 4.10 makes it evident that like preceding two analyses in the present analysis also the VBTC teachers have once again been observed to posses a higher level of teaching competency than their counter parts possessing other than VBTC training. Mean score obtained by VBTC teachers on 'Transactional' dimension of teaching competency is 15.02 as compared to only 14.02, 11.53 and 9.00 obtained by teachers having B.T.C., J.B.T. and B.Ed. training respectively.

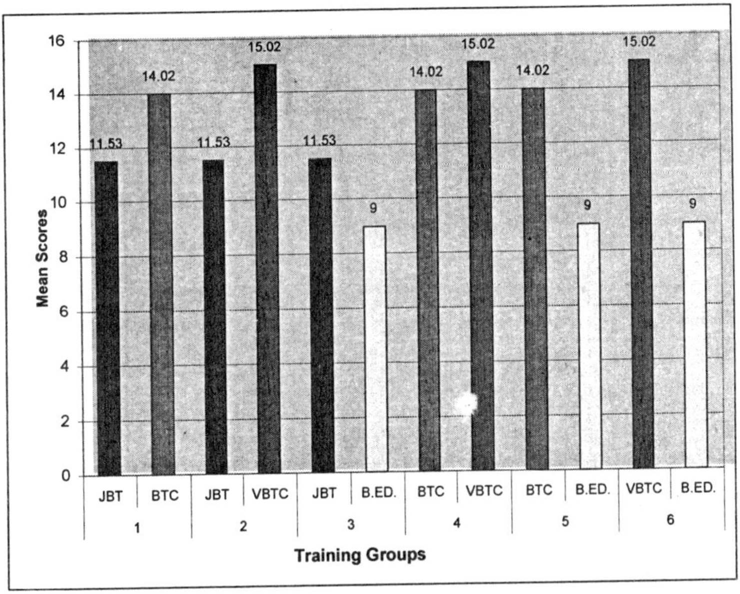

Fig. 4.10. Mean scores on 'Transactional' dimension of Teaching Competency obtained by different Training groups of teachers

To see the significance of difference between the various comparison groups, the table reveals that out of the six comparisons, in three comparisons the mean differences are observed to be significant. These are (1) B.T.C. vs. J.B.T. in which B.T.Cs. have surpassed the J.B.Ts., (2) J.B.T. vs. V.B.T.C. in which V.B.T.Cs. have excelled the JBTs, and (3) VBTC vs. B.Ed. in which VBTCs have scored higher than B.Eds. In rest of the comparisons the t-ratios are not found to be statistically significant.

Thus, it may be concluded that the primary school teachers having BTC or VBTC training are better than their counterparts having JBT and B.Ed. training on the Transactional dimension of the Teaching Competency.

4.4.4 Content Competency

The next analysis is regarding the 'Content' aspect of the teaching competency. In this analysis an attempt has been made to see if the pre-service professional training received by the sampled primary school teachers is associated with their teaching competency (content dimension). The relevant data in this regard are reported in table 4.11 and also graphically presented in figure 4.11.

Table 4.11. Training-Wise Comparison of Teachers for their Teaching Competency (Content)

Teaching Competency	*Training*	*N*	*Mean*	*Std. Deviation*	*Std.Error Difference*	*t - Value*
	JBT	19	28.58	10.21	2.90	.60
	BTC	127	30.34	12.02		
	JBT	19	28.58	10.21	3.25	.89
	VBTC	50	31.48	12.71		
	JBT	19	28.58	10.21	6.46	.32
	B.ED.	4	26.50	18.41		
Content	BTC	127	30.34	12.02	2.09	.54
	VBTC	50	31.48	12.71		
	BTC	127	30.34	12.02	6.20	.61
	B.ED.	4	26.50	18.41		
	VBTC	50	31.48	12.71	6.81	.73
	B.ED.	4	26.50	18.41		

* = $p < 0.05$

* *= $p < 0.01$

It may be noted from perusal of table 4.11 that there is no significant difference in the mean scores obtained on 'content' dimension of 'Teaching Competency' by teachers holding various professional degrees / certificates. The highest mean score (31.48) is obtained by teachers holding VBTC qualification followed by those having received BTC (Mean score 30.34). JBT (Mean score 28.58) and B.Ed. (Mean score 26.50) training. Although the trend in the data suggests that the teachers having received VBTC pre-service training have scored higher than all other compared groups. BTCs have surpassed the JBTs and B.Eds., and JBTs have excelled the B.Eds. On the 'content' dimension of the 'Teaching Competency Test', yet the mean differences between these groups fail to reach the level of statistical significance.

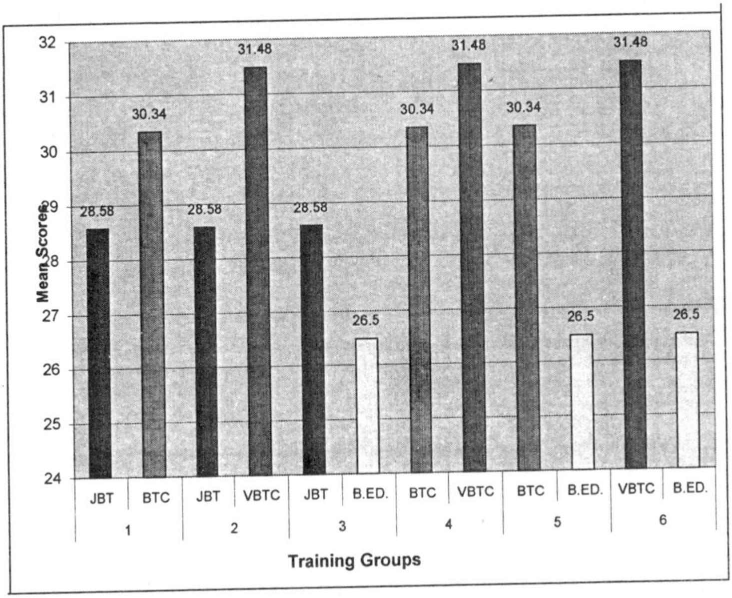

Fig. 4.11. Mean scores on 'Content' dimension of Teaching Competency obtained by different Training groups of teachers

Hence, it may be safely concluded that pre-service profession trainings of various kinds do not seem to have any differential effect on the 'content' dimension of the 'Teaching Competency' of the primary school teachers.

4.4.5 Competency of Development of Teaching-Learning Material

There can be no denying the fact that development of teaching-learning material constitutes a very important aspect of teaching competency especially at the elementary school level. The children at this stage are too young to grasp abstract ideas too easily. What is needed, therefore, at this stage that the teachers must possess at an adequate level the competency in developing effective, interesting and also low-cost teaching-learning materials for children? To generate competency in developing these materials is also considered as an important aspect of the teacher training programmes both at the pre-service and in-service levels.

Here in the next analysis an attempt has been made to relate competency in development of teaching-learning material with the pre-service professional trainings of different kinds being imparted to elementary school teachers now a days. The relevant data in this regard are summarized in table 4.12 and also graphically presented in figure 4.12.

Table 4.12. Training-Wise Comparison of Teachers for their Teaching Competency (Development of Teaching-Learning Material)

Teaching Competency	*Training*	*N*	*Mean*	*Std. Deviation*	*Std. Error Difference*	*t - Value*
	JBT	19	11.63	7.21	1.85	.05
	BTC	127	11.74	7.57		
	JBT	19	11.63	7.21	2.77	.27
	VBTC	50	12.26	8.85		
	JBT	19	11.63	7.21	3.93	.22
	B.ED.	4	10.75	6.65		
Development of Teaching Learning Material	BTC	127	11.74	7.57	1.42	.36
	VBTC	50	12.26	8.85		
	BTC	127	11.74	7.57	3.83	.25
	B.ED.	4	10.75	6.65		
	VBTC	50	12.26	8.85	4.54	.33
	B.ED.	4	10.75	6.65		

* = $p < 0.05$

* *= $p < 0.01$

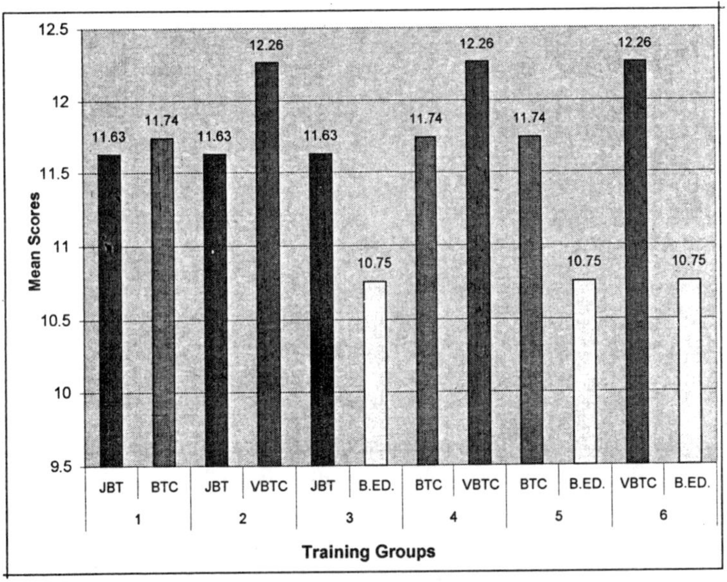

Fig. 4.12. Mean scores on 'Development of Teaching-Learning Material' dimension of Teaching Competency obtained by different Training groups of teachers

Perusal of table 4.12 and also figure 4.12 reveals that the mean scores obtained by different comparison groups of teachers range from 10.75 (for B.Ed. trained) to 12.26 (for VBTCs). BTC and JBT trained teachers occupy an intermediary position with mean scores of 11.74 and 11.63 respectively. Another fact to be noted from the table and the figure under reference is that none of the 6 t-values has turned out to be significant statistically as they vary from .05 for comparison between JBT and BTC trained teachers to .36 for comparison between BTC and VBTC trained teachers.

Thus the conclusion that emerges from this analysis is that all the four categories of teachers stand on equal footing regarding their teaching competency for development of teaching-learning material and that there is no significant difference between them in this regard. A plausible explanation for this finding may be that this is due to the fact that they all have received professional training of one kind or the other in all of which due emphasis is laid on the development of the competency in question.

To turn to the judgment on the Hypothesis – 4 of this study which anticipated 'no significant in mean scores of teaching competency of primary school teachers with respect to their training' it may be noted that this hypothesis is partially accepted and partially rejected as stated below:

1. In case of comparison between JBT and BTC trained teachers the null hypothesis was rejected for 'Educational Activities' and 'Transactional' dimensions of the Teaching Competency Test. On both these dimensions the BTC trained teachers were observed to posses greater teaching competency than JBT trained teachers. On other 3 dimensions of this test the null hypothesis was accepted.

2. In case of comparison between JBT and VBTC trained teachers also the null hypothesis was rejected for 'Educational Activities' and 'Transactional' dimensions of teaching competency. On both these dimensions the VBTC trained teachers were found to possess greater teaching competency than JBT trained teacher. On other three dimensions of Teaching Competency namely, contextual, content and development of teaching-learning material both the groups of teachers were found to be equal.

3. In case of comparison between JBT and B.Ed. groups of teachers the null hypothesis is accepted for all the dimensions of teaching competency. On all the five dimensions of Teaching Competency Test these two groups of teachers were found to posses almost equal level of teaching competency.

4. In case of comparison between BTC and VBTC trained teachers the null hypothesis was rejected for 'Educational Activities' dimension of teaching competency. On this dimension of Teaching Competency Test VBTC trained teacher were found to be significantly more competent than BTC trained teachers. On all other dimensions the null hypothesis is accepted.
5. In case of comparison between BTC and B.Ed. trained teachers the null hypothesis is accepted on all the five dimensions at teaching competency. On all the 5 dimensions, these two groups were found to be equal in teaching competency.
6. In case of comparison between VBTC and B.Ed. trained teachers the null hypothesis was rejected for 'Educational Activities' and 'Transactional' dimensions and accepted for rest of the dimensions of the teaching competency. On 'Educational Activities' as well as 'Transactional' dimensions of the Teaching Competency Test, the VBTC trained teachers were found to possess significantly greater teaching competency than B.Ed. trained teachers.

4.5 HABITAT-WISE ANALYSIS OF TEACHING COMPETENCY

Objective 5 of this study was to compare the teaching competency of primary school teachers with respect to their habitat'. Relating to this objective, the researcher formulated the following hypothesis:

H_5 "There is no significant difference in mean scores of teaching competency of primary school teachers with respect to their habitat."

To realize the aforesaid objective and test the concerned hypothesis, Mean, S.D. and t-ratios were computed for rural and urban teachers on the basis of scores obtained by them on each of the five dimensions of the 'Teaching Competency Test' developed and used by the investigator in the present study. The results thus obtained are exhibited in table 4.13. Figure 4.13 further depicts these results.

Table 4.13. Habitat -wise comparison of Teachers for Their Teaching Competencies

Teaching Competencies	*Habitat*	*N*	*Mean*	*Std. Deviation*	*Std. Error Difference*	*t-Value*
Educational Activities	Rural	100	47.85	8.66	1.18	.42
	Urban	100	48.35	8.14		
Contextual	Rural	100	7.04	2.34	.30	1.31
	Urban	100	7.44	1.92		
Transactional	Rural	100	13.41	4.82	.64	1.60
	Urban	100	14.45	4.33		
Content	Rural	100	29.04	13.02	1.70	1.57
	Urban	100	31.72	11.03		
Development of Teaching Learning Material	Rural	100	10.40	8.48	1.09	2.64**
	Urban	100	13.28	6.84		
Total Teaching Competency	Rural	100	108.04	29.25	3.88	1.91
	Urban	100	115.50	25.62		

* = $p < 0.05$
* *= $p < 0.01$

It is readily perceived from table 4.13 that except one dimension of teaching competency, namely, 'Development of Teaching-Learning Material', no significant difference is noted between the mean scores obtained by rural and urban teachers. Both the groups are observed to be almost equal on 'Educational Activities', 'Contextual', Transactional' and 'Content' dimensions of teaching competency. Even for total teaching competency the t-value for the two comparison groups has not reached the .05 level of significance. This means that habitat (i.e. residential background) of the teacher is not an important factor influencing his overall teaching competency but it is certainly an important factor for 'Development of Teaching Learning Material' component of his teaching competency as urban teachers in this analysis are observed to be significantly more competent than their counterparts residing in rural setting.

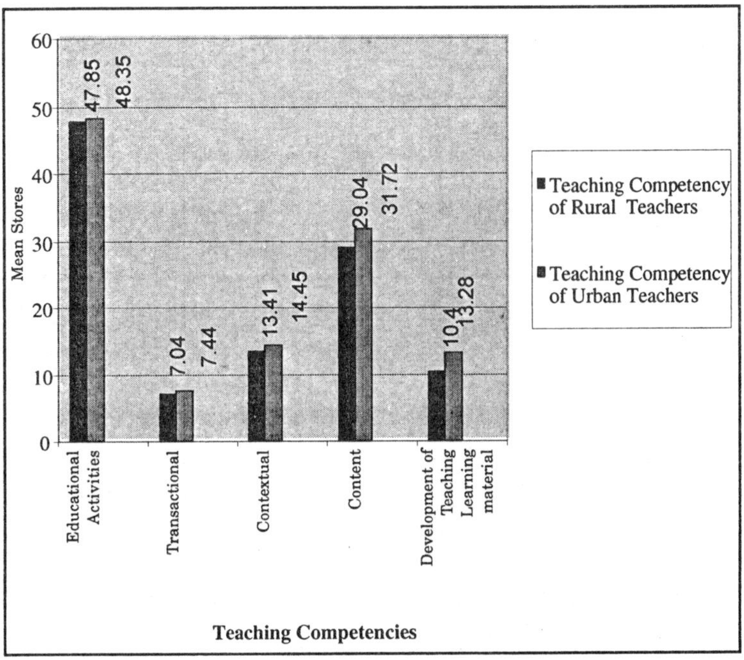

Fig. 4.13. Mean scores on Teaching Competency obtained by rural and urban Primary School Teachers

In conclusion, the hypothesis 5 of this study that "There is no significant difference in mean scores of teaching competency of primary school teachers with respect to their habitat" is accepted only partially. Out of the 5 dimensions of Teaching Competency Test, significant difference between rural and urban teachers could be observed only on one dimension namely, 'Development of Teaching-Learning Material'. On this dimension the urban teachers scored significantly higher mean score than the rural teachers. On the other 4 dimensions of the Teaching Competency Test and also for Total Teaching Competency the two groups of rural and urban teachers were observed to posses almost equal level of teaching competency.

4.6 TEACHING EXPERIENCE-WISE ANALYSIS OF TEACHING COMPETENCY

Objective – 6 of the present study proposed a comparison between teachers with different teaching experience. Related with this objective the investigator formulated the following null hypothesis:

H_6. "There is no significant difference in mean scores of teaching competency of primary school teachers with respect to their teaching experience."

To meet the above objective and verify the concerned null hypothesis, the sampled teachers were first divided into three groups for the purposes of comparison as under:

1. Teachers having up to 10 years of teaching experience.
2. Teachers with 10 to 20 years of teaching experience.
3. Teachers with more than 20 years of teaching experience.

Thereafter, Mean, S.D., t-ratios etc. were computed for the different comparison groups on the basis of teaching competency scores obtained by them as shown in tables 4.14 to 4.18. Figures 4.14 to 4.18 further depict comparative pictures of mean teaching competency scores obtained by these groups.

4.6.1 Competency of Educational Activities

Table 4.14 summarizes the data with regard to 'Educational Activities' dimension of the teaching competency for the different experience groups of teachers. Figure 4.14 further illustrates the position.

Table 4.14. Teaching Experience-wise comparison of Teachers for Their Teaching Competency (Educational Activities)

Teaching Compe-tency	*Experience*	*N*	*Mean*	*Std. Deviation*	*Std. Error Diffe-rence*	*t-Value*
Educational Activities	1 to 10 Years	114	49.84	7.93	1.60	.56
	10 – 20 Years	28	48.93	6.07		
	1 to 10 Years	114	49.84	7.93	1.40	3.96**
	Above 20 Years	58	44.28	9.06		
	10 – 20 Years	28	48.93	6.07	1.89	2.45*
	Above 20 Years	58	44.28	9.06		

* = $p < 0.05$
* *= $p < 0.01$

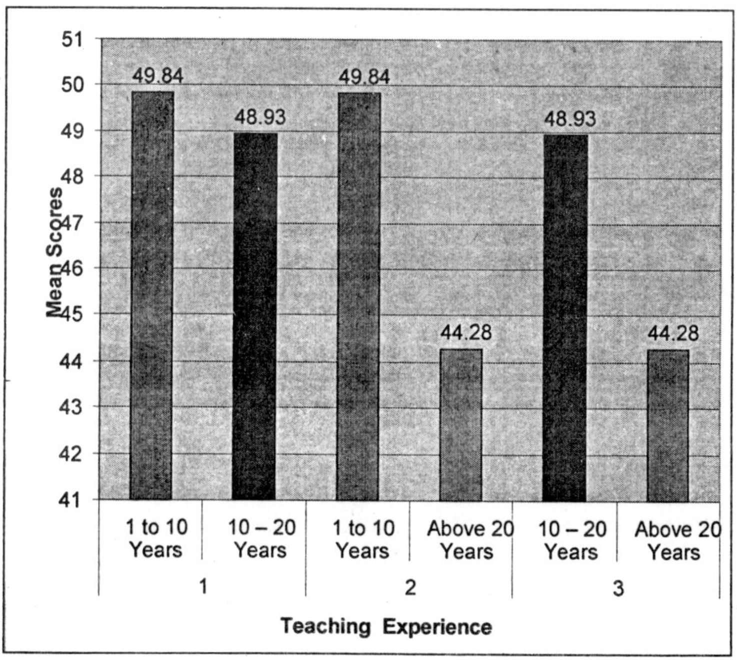

Fig. 4.14. Mean scores on 'Educational Activities' dimension of Teaching Competency obtained by different experience groups of teachers

An observation of table 4.14 makes it clear that the mean score on 'Educational Activities' aspect of Teaching Competency obtained by teachers having up to 10 years of Teaching experience is 49.84 while for teachers between 10 to 20 years of teaching experience it is 48.93 which is not significantly different from the former (t-ratio .56). This means that these two comparison groups have almost the same level of teaching competency in Educational Activities.

However, sharp differences are noticed between teachers with less than 10 years of teaching experience and those with more than 20 years of teaching experience. Mean scores on 'Educational Activities' dimension of Teaching Competency Test obtained by these two groups are 49.84 and 44.28 respectively. The computed t-ratio for the difference between these two means is 3.96 which is observed to be significant at 0.01 level of significance. This means that the teachers with up to 10 years of teaching experience are observed to possess significantly more teaching competence in educational activities than the teachers with more than 20 years of teaching experience.

Similarly, significant difference (t-ratio 2.45) is observed in the mean scores obtained by the teachers with 10-20 years of teaching experience (Mean score 48.93) and those with more than 20 years teaching experience (Mean score 44.28). Here also the less experience teachers are observed to possess more teaching competence than the more experience ones.

This finding is rather interesting. With the growing teaching experience the teaching competency is observed to decrease. What may be the reason behind this? A plausible explanation for this may be the gradual loss of vitality and also the lack of interest with the growing age. Decreasing impact of the pre-service training with increasing age may also be a reason. However, such hypotheses would need further probe and verification.

4.6.2. Contextual Competency

The next analysis is carried out for 'Contextual' aspect of teaching competency. The relevant data in this regard are presented in table 4.15. Figure 4.15 is the graphical presentation of the mean scores obtained by the different comparison groups of teachers formed on the basis of their teaching experience.

Table 4.15. Teaching Experience-wise comparison of Teachers for Their Teaching Competency (Contextual)

Teaching Compe-tency	*Experience*	*N*	*Mean*	*Std. Devia-tion*	*Std. Error Difference*	*t-Value*
Contextual	1 to 10 Years	114	7.54	1.88	.42	.25
	10 – 20 Years	28	7.43	2.47		
	1 to 10 Years	114	7.54	1.88	.35	2.71**
	Above 20 Years	58	6.57	2.34		
	10 – 20 Years	28	7.43	2.47	.55	1.56
	Above 20 Years	58	6.57	2.34		

* = $p < 0.05$
* *= $p < 0.01$

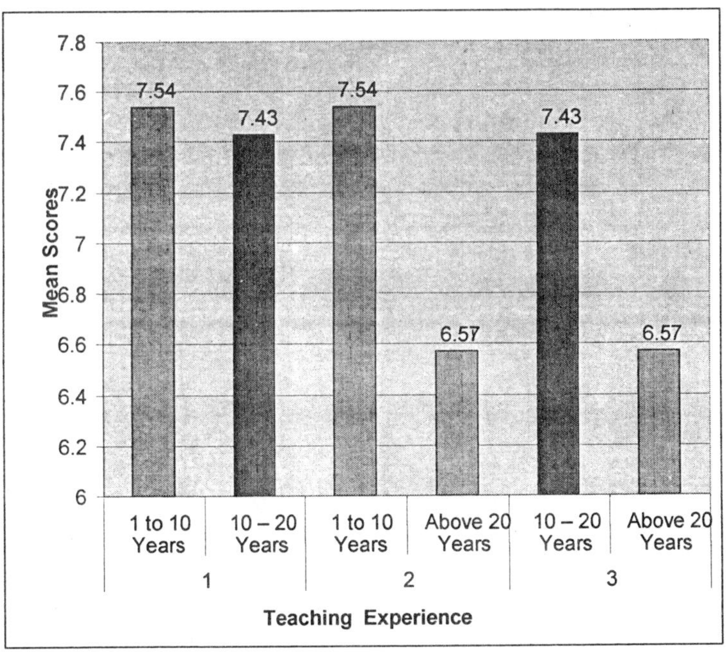

Fig. 4.15. Mean scores on 'Contextual' dimension of Teaching Competency obtained by different experience groups of teachers

A look at table 4.15 reveals that out of the three comparisons made between teachers with differing experiences of teaching in only one comparison the difference between mean scores for 'contextual' dimension of Teaching Competency has turned out to be statistically significant. This comparison is between the teachers with up to 10 years of teaching experience and those with more than 20 years of teaching experience. The mean scores obtained by these two groups are 7.54 and 6.57 respectively. The computed t-ratio for this difference in means is 2.71 which is significant at 0.01 level of significance. Like preceding analysis, in this analysis also the less experienced younger teachers are observed to have higher teaching competency than more experienced older teachers.

In other two comparisons the t-values have not reached the level of significance, hence it is concluded that the length of teaching experience has failed to show any impact on teaching competency of these groups and that these groups of teacher have almost equal level of teaching competency.

4.6.3. Transactional Competency

The next analysis is in regard to 'Transactional' aspect of teaching competency. Mean, S.D. and other statistical details pertaining to scores obtained by different experience groups of teachers on 'transaction' dimension of the Teaching Competency Test developed by the investigator are presented in table 4.16. Figure 4.16 further depicts graphically the comparative position of mean scores of different groups.

Table 4.16. Teaching Experience-wise comparison of Teachers for Their Teaching Competency (Transactional)

Teaching Competency	*Experience*	*N*	*Mean*	*Std. Deviation*	*Std. Error Difference*	*t-Value*
Transactional	1 to 10 Years	114	14.94	4.70	.97	.67
	10 – 20 Years	28	14.29	4.21		
	1 to 10 Years	114	14.94	4.70	.67	4.72**
	Above 20 Years	58	11.78	3.84		
	10 – 20 Years	28	14.29	4.21	.91	2.74**
	Above 20 Years	58	11.78	3.84		

* = $p < 0.05$ ** = $p < 0.01$

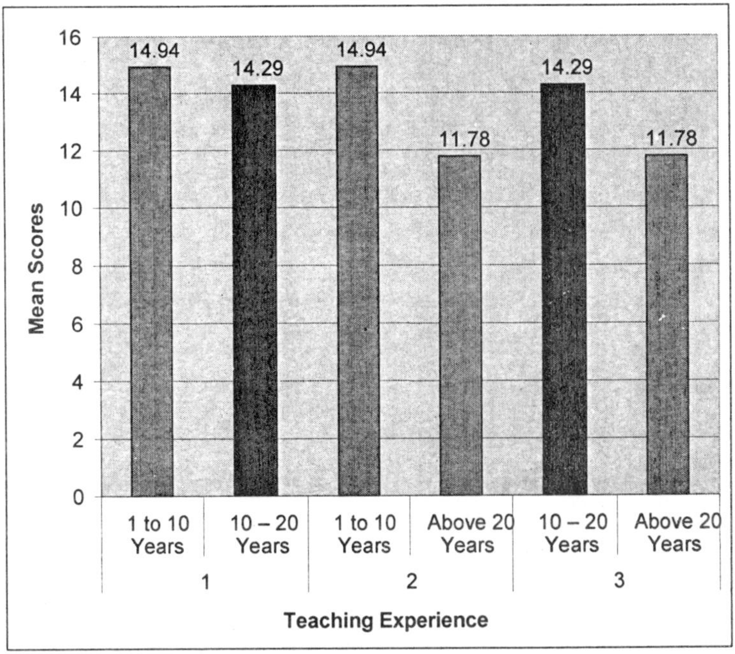

Fig. 4.16. Mean scores on 'Transactional' dimension of Teaching Competency obtained by different experience groups of teachers

It may be readily noted from a look at the table 4.16 that the highest mean score (14.94) on 'transactional' teaching competency is obtained by teachers having up to 10 years of teaching experience followed by those with 10-20 years of teaching experience (14.29). The lowest mean score (11.78) is obtained by those with above 20 years of teaching experience. This is the same trend as noted in the preceding two analyses.

As regards the significance of difference between the mean scores of different groups, the table makes it clear that out of the three comparisons made, in two comparisons the differences in mean scores have reached the level of significance. One of these is the comparison between teachers with up to 10 years experience and those with more than 20 years experience (t-value 4.72). This difference in mean scores between them is found significant at .01 level of significance. The other comparison yielding a t-value of 2.74, is also found significant at .01 level of confidence. This comparison is between teacher with up to 10 years of experience and those with above 20 years of teaching experience.

Thus it may be safely concluded that the younger and less experienced the teachers, the more is their Transactional teaching competency.

4.6.4. Content Competency

Relevant data on 'Content' dimension of teaching competency for sampled teachers having different lengths of teaching experience are exhibited in table 4.17. Figure 4.17 further depicts the graphical form of the mean scores obtained by the different comparison groups.

Table 4.17. Teaching Experience-wise comparison of Teachers for Their Teaching Competency (Content)

Teaching Compe-tency	*Experience*	*N*	*Mean*	*Std. Devia-tion*	*Std. Error Difference*	*t-Value*
Content	1 to 10 Years	114	31.01	12.82	2.57	1.27
	10 – 20 Years	28	34.29	9.18		
	1 to 10 Years	114	31.01	12.82	1.91	1.96*
	Above 20 Years	58	27.26	11.32		
	10 – 20 Years	28	34.29	9.18	2.45	2.85**
	Above 20 Years	58	27.26	11.32		

* = $p < 0.05$
* *= $p < 0.01$

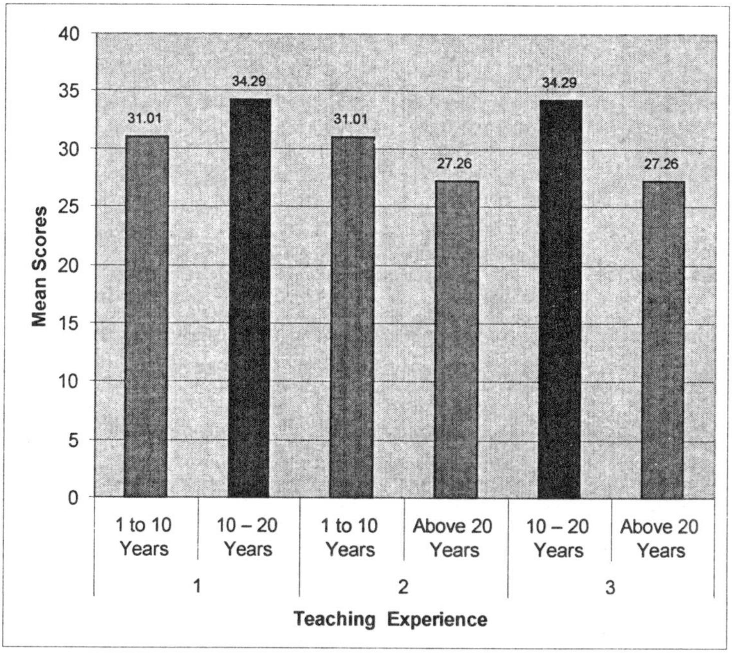

Fig. 4.17. Mean scores on 'Content' dimension of Teaching Competency obtained by different experience groups of teachers

A careful observation of table 4.17 reveals that in this analysis the highest mean score (34.29) is obtained by the teachers having 10 to 20 years of teaching experience followed by teachers with up to 10 years of experience (Mean score 31.01) and those with above 20 years of teaching experience (Mean score 27.26). While in the first comparison (between teachers with up to 10 years and 10-20 years of experience) the difference in mean scores has not been found to be statistically significant (t-value 1.27), in the second comparison (between teachers having up to 10 years and above 20 years experience) the difference in mean scores has been found to be significant at .05 level of confidence. Further, in the comparison between teachers having 10 to 20 years experience and those with more than

20 years experience the difference in mean scores is observed significant at 0.01 level of significance.

Thus the conclusion emerging from the above analysis is that on the 'Content' dimension of the Teaching Competency comparatively less experienced teachers are observed to exhibit a greater amount of teaching competency in comparison with more experienced teachers.

4.6.5. Competency of Development of Teaching-Learning Material

In the series of teaching experience-wise analysis of teaching competency, the last analysis is regarding competency in development of teaching-learning material. The relevant data in this regard are presented in table 4.18. Figure 4.18 adumbrates the mean scores obtained by different comparison groups on the teaching competency under reference.

Table 4.18. Teaching Experience-wise comparison of Teachers for Their Teaching Competency (Development of Teaching-Learning Material)

Teaching Compe- tency	*Experience*	*N*	*Mean*	*Std. Devia- tion*	*Std. Error Difference*	*t-Value*
Development	1 to 10 Years	114	11.92	8.12	1.68	2.17*
of Teaching	10 – 20 Years	28	15.57	7.32		
Learning	1 to 10 Years	114	11.92	8.12	1.17	1.73
Material	Above 20 Years	58	9.88	6.82		
	10 – 20 Years	28	15.57	7.32	1.60	3.54**
	Above 20 Years	58	9.88	6.82		

* = $p < 0.05$
* *= $p < 0.01$

Table 4.18 presents a somewhat different picture than what is observed in case of other analysis based on teaching experience of teachers reported in tables 4.14 to 4.17. Here, unlike the preceding 4 analyses, no significant difference is observed between mean scores of teachers with up to

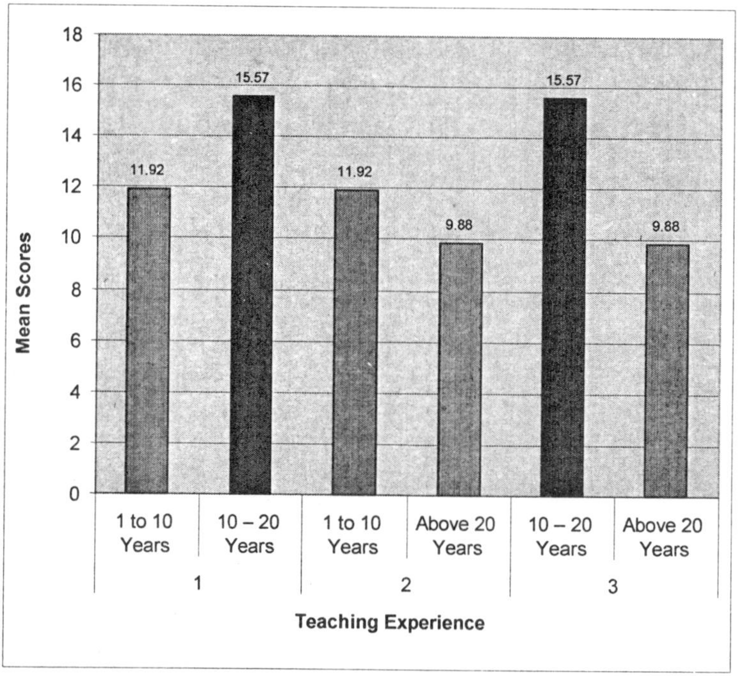

Fig. 4.18. Mean scores on 'Development of Teaching-Learning Material' dimension of Teaching Competency obtained by different experience groups of teachers

10 years of teaching experience and those with more than 20 years of teaching experience. Further, mean achievement score of teachers with up to 10 years of teaching experience on the 'Development of Teaching-learning' dimension of Teaching Competency Test is observed in this analysis to be only 11.92 as compared to 15.57 scored by the group of teachers with 10 to 20 years of teaching experience. This mean score of 15.57 is highest among all the three comparison groups in the present analysis. This finding seems to suggest that for development of competency in teaching-learning material probably a minimum teaching experience is pre-requisite and that beyond a certain span of teaching experience this competency tends to decrease.

On the basis of the finding under discussion this minimum teaching experience may be fixed around 10 years which probably tends to decrease beyond 20 years of experience.

Thus, to conclude on this section and decide upon the hypothesis-6 of this study, it may be stated that the aforesaid hypothesis expected "no significant difference in mean scores of teaching competency of primary school teachers with respect to their teaching experience." The null hypothesis could be retained only partially as under:

1. In case of comparison between teachers with up to 10 years of teaching experience and those with 10 to 20 years of teaching experience the null hypotheses could not be retained for 'Development of Teaching-Learning Material' dimension of Teaching Competency. On this dimension of teaching competency the younger group of teachers having up to 10 years of teaching experience was observed to have significantly greater teaching competency than the older teachers with 10 to 20 years of teaching experience." On rest of the four dimension of teaching competence null hypothesis was retained.
2. In case of comparison between teachers with up to 10 years of teaching experience and those with more than 20 years of experience, the null hypothesis could be retained only for 'Development of Teaching-Learning Material' aspect of teaching competency. On this dimension of Teaching Competency Test, both the comparison groups of teachers were found to possess almost equal level of teaching competency. For rest of the four dimensions of teaching competency namely, educational activities, contextual, transactional and content, the null hypothesis was rejected. On these 4 dimensions of Teaching Competency Test, the teachers having only up to 10 years of teaching experience were observed

to have significantly greater teaching competency than teachers with more than 20 years of teaching experience.

3. In case of comparison between teachers with 10-20 years of teaching experience and those with more than 20 years of teaching experience, the null hypothesis could be retained only for 'contextual' dimension of teaching competency. On this dimension of teaching competency the two comparison groups were found to be equal. For rest of the 4 aspects of teaching competency namely, Educational Activities, Transactional, Content and Development of Teaching-Learning Material, the null hypothesis was rejected. On these four dimensions of Teaching Competency Test, the younger group of teachers having only up to 10 years of teaching experience proved to possess significantly greater teaching competency than the teachers with more than 20 years of teaching experience.

4.7 ACADEMIC STREAM-WISE ANALYSIS OF TEACHING COMPETENCY:

Objective – 7 of the present study was to "Compare the teaching competency of primary school teachers with respect to their academic stream, i.e. Science, Arts and Commerce." Related to this objective, the investigator formulated the following hypothesis:

H_6 "There is no significant difference in mean scores of teaching competency of primary school teachers with respect to their academic stream."

To meet the aforesaid objective and test the related hypothesis on the basis of empirical data, it was required to compare the mean scores obtained by teachers belonging to different academic streams on Teaching Competency Test developed and used by the investigator in this study.

Computation of Mean, S.D., t-ratio and other relevant statistics was also required for this purpose which are reported in Tables 4.19 – 4.23 and further depicted graphically in figures 4.19-4.23.

4.7.1 Competency of Educational Activities

Relevant data pertaining to competency of 'Educational Activities' are presented in Table 4.19. Figure 4.19 further illustrates graphically the mean scores obtained by the different comparison groups.

Table 4.19. Academic Stream-wise comparison of Teachers for Their Teaching Competency (Educational Activities)

Teaching Competency	*Academic Stream*	*N*	*Mean*	*Std. Deviation*	*Std. Error Difference*	*t-Value*
Educational Activities	Science	52	50.73	8.35	1.36	2.71**
	Arts	135	47.02	8.40		
	Science	52	50.73	8.35	2.68	.67
	Commerce	11	48.91	6.50		
	Arts	135	47.02	8.40	2.60	.72
	Commerce	11	48.91	6.50		

* = $p < 0.05$
** = $p < 0.01$

A careful look at table 4.19 makes it clear that the only comparison in this table which significantly differentiates between the two groups is that of teachers from Science and Arts streams. While the mean score obtained by the teachers of science stream on 'Educational Activities' aspect of teaching competency is observed to be 50.73 which is highest among the three comparison groups, the mean score of teachers from Arts group is only 47.02 which is lowest among the three comparison groups. This difference of 3.71 in the mean scores of the two groups under comparison (50.73-47.02) is statistically significant at .01 level of significance (t-ratio 2.71). This means that teachers belonging to science streams are significantly more competent in educational activities than their counterparts from Arts stream.

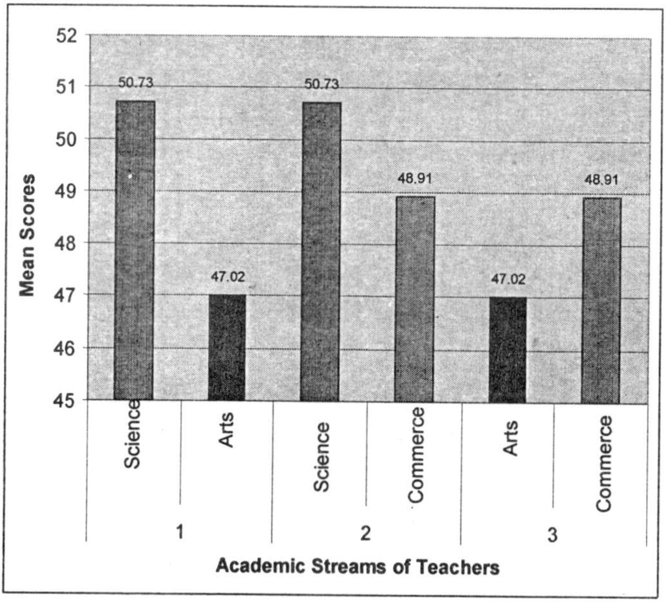

Fig. 4.19. Mean Scores on Competency of 'Educational Activities' obtained by teachers from different academic streams

As regards the comparisons between Science and Commerce streams teachers and between Arts and Commerce streams teachers, no significant difference is observed between them (t-value .67 and .72 respectively) and that those teachers posses almost equal teaching competency of 'Educational Activities'.

4.7.2 Contextual Competency

The next analysis is in regard to 'contextual' dimension of teaching competency. Here the purpose is to see which of the comparison groups stand significantly superior to others in teaching competency. These comparison groups are drawn from different academic streams, namely, Science, Arts and Commerce. The relevant data regarding these groups are exhibited in table 4.20 and also in the figure with the same number.

Table 4.20. Academic Stream-wise comparison of Teachers for Their Teaching Competency (Contextual)

Teaching Competency	*Academic Stream*	*N*	*Mean*	*Std. Deviation*	*Std. Error Difference*	*t-Value*
Contextual	Science	52	7.60	2.27	.36	1.38
	Arts	135	7.10	2.05		
	Science	52	7.60	2.27	.77	.06
	Commerce	11	7.55	2.65		
	Arts	135	7.10	2.05	.66	.68
	Commerce	11	7.55	2.65		

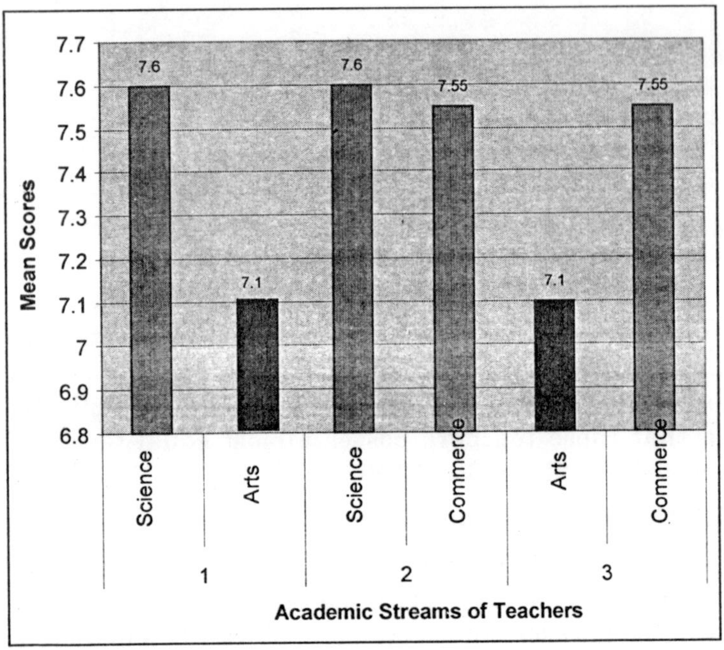

Fig. 4.20. Mean Scores on Competency of 'Contextual' obtained by teachers from different academic streams

It may be readily perceived from table 4.20 that in none of the comparisons the difference between means scores is statistically significant. Range of mean score in all the three comparisons in this table varies from 7.10 (for Arts stream) to 7.60 (for science streams). The computed t-values range between .06 and 1.38 which are not significant. Thus the null hypothesis is fully accepted in this analysis and it may be safely concluded that the academic stream of teachers is not observed to make any difference in their 'contextual' teaching competency. In other words the comparison groups are found to be almost equal in the matter of 'contextual' teaching competency.

Figure 4.20 graphically adumbrates the same position.

4.7.3 Transactional Competency

In the next analysis an attempt has been made to compare the mean scores obtained by the teachers of different academic streams on transactional aspect of teaching competency. The objective behind this comparison is to see if the academic stream of the teacher is an important factor in determining his/her teaching competency. The relevant data in this regard are presented in table 4.21 and figure 4.21 depicts the mean scores of different groups graphically.

Table 4.21. Academic Stream-wise comparison of Teachers for Their Teaching Competency (Transactional)

Teaching Compe-tency	*Academic Stream*	*N*	*Mean*	*Std. Devia-tion*	*Std. Error Difference*	*t-Value*
Transac-tional	Science	52	15.37	4.15	.69	2.69**
	Arts	135	13.49	4.53		
	Science	52	15.37	4.15	1.52	1.66
	Commerce	11	12.82	6.41		
	Arts	135	13.49	4.53	1.47	.45
	Commerce	11	12.82	6.41		

* = $p < 0.05$

** = $p < 0.01$

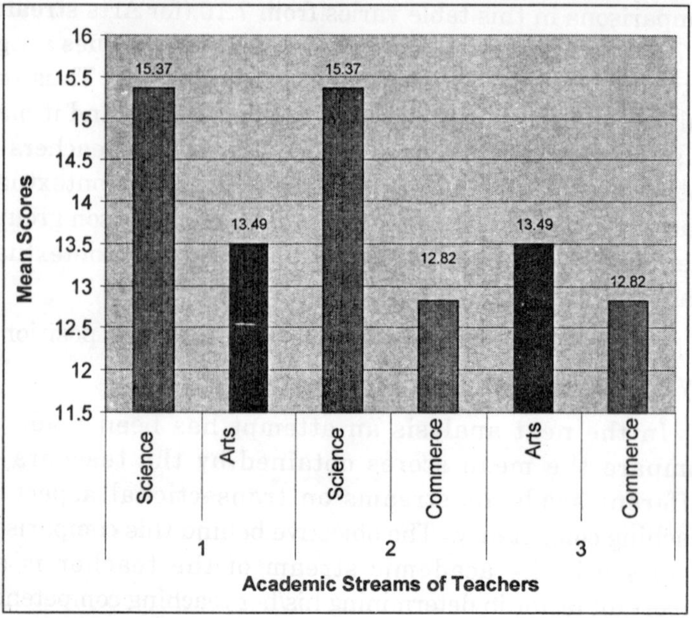

Fig. 4.21. Mean Scores on Competency of 'Transactional' obtained by teachers from different academic streams.

Perusal of table 4.21 and also figure 4.21 reveals that the highest mean score (15.37) is obtained by teachers of science stream followed by teachers of Arts Stream (13.49) and commerce stream (12.82) respectively. However, it is only the comparison between Science and Arts groups in which the difference in mean scores is observed to be significant at .01 level of significance (t-value 2.69). In rest of the two comparisons the mean differences have failed to reach the level of significance.

Thus it may be concluded on the basis of the present analysis that the teachers belonging to Science Stream are observed to be significantly more competent than the teachers from Arts Stream in the 'transactional' competency while no significant differences could be observed between teachers belonging to (a) Science and Commerce group and (b) Arts and Commerce group in the matter of this competency.

4.7.4 Content Competency

For comparison of 'Content' competency among teachers belonging to different academic streams, the required data are summarized in table 4.22. Figure 4.22 further depicts the mean scores of the comparison groups graphically.

Table 4.22. Academic Stream-wise comparison of Teachers for Their Teaching Competency (Content)

Teaching Competency	*Academic Stream*	*N*	*Mean*	*Std. Deviation*	*Std. Error Difference*	*t-Value*
Content	Science	52	33.12	11.31	1.88	1.82
	Arts	135	29.67	12.21		
	Science	52	33.12	11.31	3.83	1.07
	Commerce	11	29.00	12.77		
	Arts	135	29.67	12.21	3.84	.17
	Commerce	11	29.00	12.77		

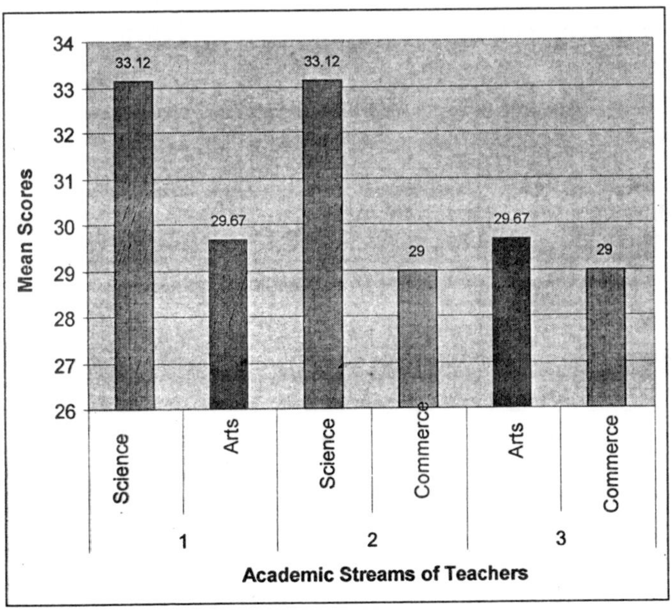

Fig. 4.22. Mean Scores on Competency of 'Content' obtained by teachers from different academic streams.

It may be readily noted from a look at table 4.22 that the highest mean score on 'Content' dimension of teaching competency (33.12) is obtained by teachers of Science Stream followed by mean score of 29.67 for Arts Stream teachers and that of 29.00 for Commerce Stream teachers. However, in none of the comparisons the mean difference is observed to be statistically significant (t-ratios computed for different comparison groups vary from .17 to 1.82).

Hence, the null hypothesis is confirmed in this analysis.

4.7.5. Competency of Development of Teaching-Learning Material

The present analysis is the last in the series of academic stream-wise analysis of teaching competency. This concerns competency in 'Development of Teaching-Learning Material'. In this analysis an attempt has been made to find out whether or not the academic steam to which the teacher belongs is an important factor responsible for his/her teaching competency in 'Development of Teaching-Learning Material'. The required data for this analysis are summarized in table 4.23. Figure 4.23 further adumbrates graphically, the mean scores on the competency under reference obtained by the teachers of different streams.

Table 4.23. Academic Stream-wise comparison of Teachers for Their Teaching Competency (Development of Teaching-Learning Material)

Teaching Competency	*Academic Stream*	*N*	*Mean*	*Std. Deviation*	*Std. Error Difference*	*t-Value*
Development	Science	52	13.17	7.54	1.25	1.41
of Teaching	Arts	135	11.41	7.98		
Learning	Science	52	13.17	7.54	2.49	1.01
Material	Commerce	11	10.64	7.29		
	Arts	135	11.41	7.98	2.48	.31
	Commerce	11	10.64	7.29		

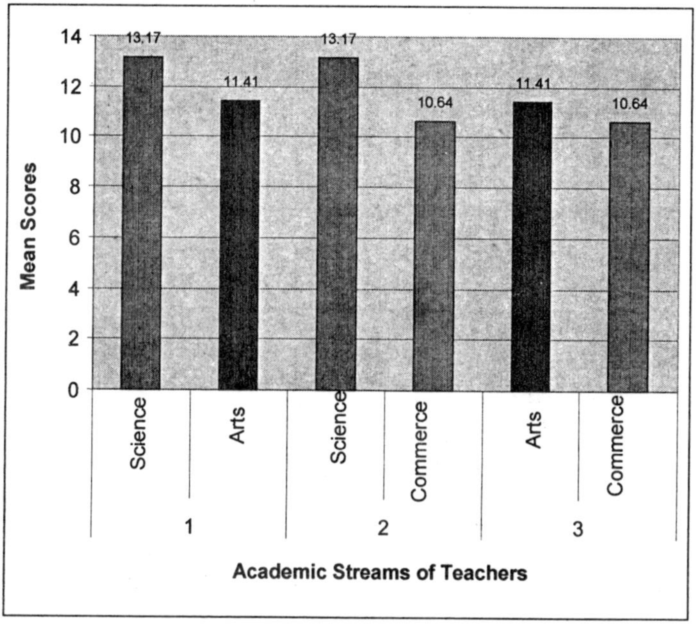

Fig. 4.23. Mean Scores on Competency of 'Development of Teaching-Learning Material' obtained by teachers from different academic streams

A careful observation of table 4.23 and also figure 4.23 reveals that although the trend in the data suggests that teachers from Science Stream have scored a higher mean (13.17) than the teachers from Arts and Commerce Streams (mean score 11.41 and 10.64 respectively) and also that teachers belonging to Arts Stream have scored a higher mean (11.41) than teachers belonging to Commerce Stream (mean=10.64), the differences between these means have failed to reach the level of statistical significance.

As such, the conclusion that flows from the above analysis is that all the three groups of teachers divided on the basis of their academic stream are observed to be equal in the competency for 'Development of Teaching-Learning Material' and that the academic-stream is not observed to have any association with this competency.

So what about the final answer to the hypothesis – 7 of this study? It may be recalled that hypothesis-7 of this study anticipated "no significant difference in mean scores of teaching competency of primary school teachers with respect to their academic stream". On the basis of the findings of this study this null hypothesis is partly accepted and partly rejected as under:

1. In case of comparison between teachers belonging to Science and Arts Streams Null hypothesis was rejected for 'Educational Activities' and 'Transactional' dimensions of Teaching Competency Test. In both these comparisons Science Stream teachers were found to possess significantly greater teaching competency than Arts Stream teachers. In comparisons for other 3 dimensions of teaching competency namely, contextual, content and development of teaching-learning material, the null hypothesis was accepted as both the comparison groups were found equal on these dimensions of Teaching Competency Test.
2. In case of comparison between teachers belonging to Science and Commerce Streams null hypothesis was accepted for all the 5 dimensions of Teaching Competency Test. On all the 5 dimensions teachers from these two streams were found to be almost equal.
3. In comparison between teachers belonging to Arts and Commerce Streams also the null hypothesis was fully accepted. On all the 5 dimensions of Teaching Competency Test these two groups were observed to possess almost equal level of teaching competency.

5

Teaching Competency of Primary School Teachers

5.1 CONCLUSIONS

On the basis of statistical analysis of the data collected in this study, the following conclusions have been arrived at:

5.1.1 Findings related to Level of Teaching Competency

57.7% (115 out of 200) teachers of primary schools are observed to have 'high' or 'very high' level of teaching competency, while 42.3% (85 out of 200) are found to have 'low' or 'very low' level of teaching competency.

Thus the hypothesis – 1 of this study which anticipated that majority of primary school teachers in Lucknow District will be found to possess 'high' / 'very high' level of teaching competency is confirmed.

5.1.2 Findings related to Gender-Wise Analysis of Teaching Competency

On all the five dimensions of teaching competency namely, 'Educational Activities', 'Contextual', 'Transactional', 'Content' and 'Development of Teaching-Learning Material', no significant difference could be observed between male and female teachers. Both the groups were found to be almost equal in terms of mean scores on all these dimensions. Also for total teaching competency, the t-value for the two groups did not reach the .05 level of significance. This shows that gender is not an important factor for teaching competency at the primary school level in Lucknow District.

Thus, the hypothesis – 2 of this study that 'There is no significant difference in the mean scores of teaching competency of primary school teachers is retained.'

5.1.3 Findings related to Academic Qualification-Wise Analysis of Teaching Competency

1. On 'Educational Activities' dimension, (a) Post-graduate qualified teachers are observed to be significantly higher than teachers with high school, intermediate and graduate qualification, (b) graduate teachers are found to be significantly more competent than teachers having high school qualification and (c) no significant difference is noticed between teachers with high school and intermediate qualification.

2. On 'Contextual' dimension, teachers with post-graduation qualification are observed to be significantly more competent than high school and intermediate pass teachers, while teachers with graduation qualification are found to be significantly more competent than intermediate and high school pass qualification. No significant difference, however, was noticed between teachers with high school and intermediate qualification and also between teachers with graduation and post graduation qualifications.

3. On 'Transactional' aspect of teaching competency, (a) teachers with post-graduate qualification scored significantly higher than teachers with graduation and high school qualifications, (b) teachers with graduation qualification scored significantly higher than high school pass teachers, and (c) no significant difference was found between high school and inter pass teachers and also between teachers with intermediate and graduation qualification.

4. On 'Content' dimension of teaching competency, no significant difference were observed between teachers with (a) high school and intermediate qualification, (b) high school and graduation qualification, and (c) intermediate and graduation qualification. However, teachers having post

graduate qualification were found to be significantly more competent than teachers with high school, intermediate and graduation qualification.

5. On 'Development of teaching-learning material' dimension of teaching competency, intermediate pass teachers were observed to possess significantly greater teaching competency than high school passed teachers while post graduate teachers were found to be significantly more competent than high school, intermediate as well as graduate teachers.

Thus, the hypothesis – 3 of this study which visualized "no significant difference in mean scores of teaching competency of primary school teachers with respect to their academic qualification" is retained only partially. In majority of analyses carried out in this regard, significant differences have been observed between teachers with varying qualifications, the general trend being that the higher the qualification, the greater the teaching competency.

5.1.4 Professional Training-Wise Analysis of Teaching Competency

1. For two dimensions namely 'Educational Activities' and 'Transactional', the BTC trained teachers were observed to possess greater teaching competency than JBT trained teachers. On remaining three dimensions of teaching competency, no effect of training is observed.

2. For 'Educational Activities' and 'Transactional' dimensions of teaching competency VBTC trained teachers were found to possess greater teaching competency than JBT trained teacher. On other three dimensions of Teaching Competency namely, contextual, content and development of teaching-learning material both the groups of teachers were found to be equal.

3. For all the five dimensions of Teaching Competency Test JBT and B.Ed. teachers were found to posses almost equal level of teaching competency.

4. For 'Educational Activities' dimension of teaching competency, VBTC trained teacher were found to be significantly more competent than BTC trained teachers. On all other dimensions, there is no effect of training.

5. On all the 5 dimensions, two groups of BTC and B.Ed. teachers were found to be equal in teaching competency.

6. On 'Educational Activities' as well as 'Transactional' dimensions of the Teaching Competency Test, the VBTC trained teachers were found to possess significantly greater teaching competency than B.Ed. trained teachers.

5.1.5 Findings related to Habitat-Wise Analysis of Teaching Competency

1. Out of the 5 dimensions of Teaching Competency Test, significant difference between rural and urban teachers could be observed only on one dimension namely, 'Development of Teaching-Learning Material'. On this dimension the urban teachers scored significantly higher mean score than the rural teachers. On the other 4 dimensions of the Teaching Competency Test and also for Total Teaching Competency the two groups of rural and urban teachers were observed to posses almost equal level of teaching competency.

5.1.6 Findings related to Teaching Experience-Wise Analysis of Teaching Competency

1. On 'Development of Teaching-Learning Material' dimension of teaching competency, the younger group of teachers having up to 10 years of teaching experience was observed to have significantly greater teaching competency than the older teachers with 10 to 20 years of teaching experience. On rest of the four dimension of teaching competence null hypothesis was retained.

2. On 'Development of Teaching-Learning Material' dimension only of Teaching Competency Test, teachers with up to 10 years of teaching experience and those with more than 20 years of experience were found to possess almost

equal level of teaching competency. On remaining four dimensions of Teaching Competency Test, the teachers having only up to 10 years of teaching experience were observed to have significantly greater teaching competency than teachers with more than 20 years of teaching experience.

3. On 'contextual' dimension of teaching competency, teachers with 10-20 years of teaching experience and those with more than 20 years of teaching experience were found to be equal. For rest of the four dimensions namely, Educational Activities, Transactional, Content and Development of Teaching-Learning Material of Teaching Competency Test, the younger group of teachers having only up to 10 years of teaching experience proved to possess significantly greater teaching competency than the teachers with more than 20 years of teaching experience.

5.1.7 Findings related to Academic Stream-Wise Analysis of Teaching Competency

1. For 'Educational Activities' and 'Transactional' dimensions of Teaching Competency Test, teachers belonging to Science Streams were found to possess significantly greater teaching competency than Arts Stream teachers. In comparisons for other 3 dimensions of teaching competency namely, contextual, content and development of teaching-learning material, both the comparison groups were found equal.

2. On all the 5 dimensions, teachers belonging to Science and Commerce Streams were found to be almost equal.

3. On all the 5 dimensions of Teaching Competency Test, teachers belonging to Arts and Commerce Streams were observed to possess almost equal level of teaching competency.

5.2 IMPLICATIONS OF FINDINGS

Following are the main implications:-

1. On the whole, level of teaching competency of only 58% teachers falls above mid point. Hence, there is need of some definite compulsory programmes of staff development, through which the in-service teachers can develop their skills and competencies. Better infrastructural facilities in government schools should also be provided to enhance competency level of their teachers. It is also essential that the concerned authorities of government schools should find out the ways to maintain the academic environment and standard of their schools, so that the competent teachers are attracted to offer their services.

2. Result reveals that there is no significant effect of gender on teaching competency of primary school teachers although the trend in the data suggests that female teachers show better performance than male teachers. As such attention should be paid during appointment of primary school teachers that proportion of male and female teachers should be equal as far as possible / practicable.

3. Results show that highly qualified teachers possess better teaching competency. As such at the time of recruitment of primary school teachers, minimum qualification should be made graduation. Also there should be provision of in-service study for primary school teachers. By this scheme teachers may increase their qualification and enhance their teaching competency. For those teachers who are trying to enhance their qualification, incentives like additional increment, promotion etc. should be provided.

4. As professional training has emerged as one of the predictors of teaching competency, it is essential to recruit only trained teachers in the schools. There should also be provision of in-service training programmes.

5. This study has also shown that teachers having longer teaching experience are not more competent than younger teachers. This implies that there should be some kind of regular teacher education programmes to keep the teachers vibrant, active and updated. The follow up

programmes should also be organized to judge the effectiveness of such programmes. Certain incentives like promotion and increment can be linked to these trainings so that the teachers compulsorily undergo these experiences and update their knowledge and skills.

5.3 SUGGESTIONS

N.C.E.R.T., S.C.E.R.T., Education For All Project Board, S.S.A. etc. and other such policy making bodies have realized the need of improvement of teaching competency of primary school teachers but the present system of improving the teaching competency is inadequate to survive in the global arena of qualitative technological information age. In order to satisfy the aspirations of the future generations the current system of teacher training is an urgent need of infrastructural overhaul.

5.3.1 Suggestions for Policy Makers

1. As the status of government school is increasingly deteriorating and there is no check or demand of accountability from the teachers, they are failing to acquire and maintain their professional standards. So there is a strong message to the government and school administrators to become alert and devise ways to improve their standard and to attract the talented teachers. Further, there should also be provision of continuous professional growth of the teachers. If the administrators of government schools become strict and keep regular check, the teachers will try best to maintain their knowledge and competencies.

2. In order to make teacher competent and effective performer of duties, it is essential to develop large network of Teacher Educational Institutions with adequate financial resources, training materials and modes.

3. There should be credibility as accorded by employment potentials to encourage attainment of competency and commitment towards the profession of teaching.

4. The infrastructural facilities in government school should be improved. Mostly the government schools are functioning in dilapidated building with no essential amenities. There is shortage of classrooms, equipments and other material. Under such circumstances teachers can not be expected to be competent. The effort should be made to provide the basic facilities to the schools. There should also be continuous evaluation of the efforts of the government made in this direction.

5. During appointment due weightage should be given to the demonstration of competencies in classroom situations.

6. Generally teachers become lethargic and do not bother for retaining their competencies, after they become permanent. So some kind of fear should be introduced. Their annual increments and promotions can be delayed if they fail to demonstrate the requisite competencies in their day to day teaching.

7. Primary school teachers should not be involved in non-teaching assignments and should not be allotted the non-academic tasks like assigning their duties during elections, vaccination and board examinations. Besides, they also be relieved from lot of paper work which they have to do in their schools.

5.3.2 Suggestions for Teacher Educators

1. Teacher education institution needs to be net-worked with a view to share resources, materials, expertise and experiences in the form teacher education complexes to undertake innovative programmes for updating and upgrading teacher education competencies.

2. In extension to networking, there needs to be provisions of study tours for pupil teachers to different centers of B.Ed./BTC institutions for insightful learning and orientation of different training programmes.

3. Training of teachers must be modern and concurrent and to achieve this, there needs to be promotion of linguistic

skill, both in Hindi and English medium to open new vistas of knowledge. The preparation and utilization of teaching aids, utilization of hardware and media such as television and computers, multimedia projects and demonstration of experiments needs to be practiced and trained.

4. Teacher training institutes should have formal attachments with co-operating schools to facilitate quality teaching experience.

5. Instructional strategies need to aim for innovations and creativity within the parameters of time duration for classroom teaching.

6. There needs to be opportunities for pupil teachers to observe good teachers at work and to participate with experienced practitioners in teaching.

7. Pupil teachers need to practice in simulated situations such as peer teaching for effective feedback and mutual learning.

5.3.3 Suggestions for Further Research

1. Future researchers can take up experimental research in the field of primary education to assess teaching competency of primary school teachers.

2. The present study measures the teaching competency of primary school teachers with respect to their gender, academic qualification, academic stream, habitat and teaching experience but there is scope of measuring other factors such as marital status, personality, socio-economic status etc.

3. The present study is confined to Lucknow district based on a sample of 200 teachers only. Future studies can explore further by taking a larger sample and even a wider geographical setting.

4. Similar studies can be conducted for districts other than Lucknow.

5. Similar studies can also be undertaken at secondary and senior secondary levels.

Appendix-A

निर्देश :

1. यह परीक्षण शोध से सम्बन्धित है। अतः आपसे पूर्ण सहयोग की अपेक्षा है।
2. प्रश्न पत्र के कई भाग हैं। प्रत्येक भाग के सभी प्रश्न करना अनिवार्य है।
3. निर्देशों को भलीभांति पढ़कर ही निर्धारित स्थान पर उत्तर लिखिये।
4. आपके उत्तर पूर्णतया गोपनीय रखे जायेंगे, अतः निःसंकोच उत्तर दीजिये।

शिक्षक/शिक्षिका का नाम : ....

विद्यालय का नाम : ....

ब्लाक : .... एन0 पी0 आर0 सी0 ....

आयु : ....

पुरूष/महिला : ....

शिक्षण अनुभव : .... वर्ष .... माह

खण्ड – 1

निर्देश : इस भाग में विद्यालयीय तथा शैक्षिक परिस्थितियों से सम्बन्धित कथन दिए हुए हैं, हम यह जानना चाहते हैं कि आप इनमें से प्रत्येक कथन से किस सीमा तक सहमति रखते हैं। यदि आप किसी कथन से पूर्णतया सहमत हैं तो उसके सम्मुख बने को ठक में '5' लिख दें तथा यदि पूर्णतया असहमत हैं तो अंक '1' लिख दें। इसी प्रकार सहमत के लिए '4',अनिश्चित के लिए '3' तथा असहमत के लिए '2' लिखें। संकेत – पूर्णतया सहमत – 5, सहमत – 4, अनिश्चित – 3, असहमत –2, पूर्णतया असहमत –1

1- प्राथमिक विद्यालयों की स्थिति ऐसी नही है कि वहॉ कोई नवाचार प्रयोग किया जा सके। []

2- क्रियाकलाप विविधता से शिक्षक अपनी कमी छिपा सकता है। []

3- सतत मूल्यांकन से विद्यार्थियों की उपलब्धियों में कोई विशेष सुधार नही होता। []

4- रेडियो/टेलीवीजन से शिक्षण कराना चोंचले बाजी है। []

5- शिष्य के मूल्यांकन के समय पाठ्यसहगामी क्रियाओं में उसकी सफलता पर ध्यान नहीं देना चाहिए। []

6- विद्यालय के कार्यक्रमों में अभिभावकों को सम्मिलित करने से उनमें शिक्षा के प्रति लगाव पैदा होता है। []

7- शिक्षणेत्तर कार्य (जैसे पल्स पोलियो) आदि करने से शिक्षक को समुदाय के लोगों से मिलने जुलने का मौका मिलता है। []

8- आधुनिक विद्यालयों के पाठ्यक्रम में अनेक ऐसी क्रियाए सम्मिलित की जा रही हैं, जो वांछनीय नहीं हैं। []

9- सहायक सामग्री के निर्माण की जिम्मेदारी अतिरिक्त बोझ है। []

10- पढ़ाते समय अनौपचारिक बातचीत समय का दुरूपयोग है। []

11- शिक्षण में विभिन्न क्रियाकलापों का प्रयोग बच्चों को विषय वस्तु से भटकाता है। []

12- छात्र द्वारा अपने विषय को ग्रहण न करने के लिए अध्यापक दोषी होता है। []

13- ग्राम शिक्षा समितियों द्वारा शिक्षकों के कार्यो का मूल्यांकन कराना उचित है। []

14- प्रतिवर्ष चार्ट, माडल व अन्य शिक्षण सहायक सामग्रियों को सहेजना कूड़ा इकट्ठा करना है। []

खण्ड – 2

निर्देश : नीचे कुछ स्थितियां दी गई हैं जो प्रायः अध्यापक के जीवन में आती हैं। आप उन स्थितियों में स्वंय को रखकर विचार करें कि उस स्थिति में आप क्या करना चाहेंगे? दिए गए विकल्पों में से जो आपके लिए सर्वोपयुक्त हो उसी पर सही (✔) का चिन्ह लगाइये।

1- हिन्दी भाषा के पाठ 'हमारे पड़ोसी' को पढ़ाने के लिए कक्षाध्यापिका श्रीमती लीलावती ने सभी छात्रो से अपने–अपने पड़ोसी के बारे में दो–तीन पंक्तियां बोलने को कहा। अध्यापिका द्वारा किया गया यह कार्य आपके अनुसार

(i) छात्रों में अपने पड़ोसी के बारे में समझ बढ़ायेगा।

(ii) छात्रों को पड़ोसी से कटु सम्बन्धों को उजागर करने का अवसर प्रदान करेगा।

(iii) विद्यार्थियों की लेखन शैली का विकास होगा।

2- हमीरपुर गॉव के प्राथमिक विद्यालय प्रांगण में हैण्डपम्प है। विद्यालय में लगा हुआ हैण्डपम्प नजदीक होने के कारण गॉव की महिलाएं विद्यालय समय में ही पानी भरने व कभी–कभी कपड़े धोने आ जाती हैं। ऐसी स्थिति में विद्यालय के अध्यापकों को क्या करना चाहिए?

(i) उनसे बात करके विद्यालय समय से पूर्व या पश्चात् पानी भरने को कहना चाहिए।

(ii) ग्राम प्रधान से बात करके उन्हें अन्यत्र कहीं पानी की व्यवस्था करने को कहना चाहिए।

(iii) विद्यालय के गेट पर ताला डलवा देना चाहिए।

3- अध्यापक श्री मोहन लाल कई दिनों से विद्यार्थियों को गणित की एक ही विषयवस्तु को समझाने की कोशिश कर रहे थे परन्तु विद्यार्थी समझ नहीं पा रहे थे। अध्यापक महोदय चिंतित हो गये कि यदि एक ही विषयवस्तु पढ़ाने में इतना समय लगेगा तो पाठ्यक्रम कैसे पूरा होगा। इसी दौरान उन्हें 10 दिवसीय शिक्षक प्रशिक्षण कार्यक्रम में भाग लेने की सूचना मिलती है। श्री आदित्य कुमार की स्थिति में यदि आप हों तो क्या करेंगे?

(i) उन्हें अपने स्थान पर अन्य शिक्षक को भेज देना चाहिये और स्वंय पाठ्यक्रम को पूरा करना चाहिये।

(ii) प्रशिक्षण कार्यक्रम में जाना चाहिये कयोंकि हो सकता है कि वहॉ सिखाई गई विधियों से उन्हें अपनी समस्या का हल मिल जाय।

(iii) पहले विद्यालय का कार्य पूर्ण करना चाहिए उसके पश्चात् प्रशिक्षण के लिए प्रस्थान करना चाहिए।

4. विज्ञान अध्यापिका श्रीमती मंजू देवी ने पेड़–पौधे पाठ पढ़ाने के लिए चार्ट्स और माडल तैयार किये। परन्तु कक्षा में पहुँचने पर उसने देखा कि वह चार्ट्स घर पर ही भूल आयी हैं। यदि आप उनकी जगह होते तो क्या करते?

   (i) पाठ बिना चार्ट की सहायता के हीं पढ़ा देते।

   (ii) वह पाठ छोड़कर कोई अन्य पाठ पढ़ा देते।

   (iii) बच्चों को विद्यालयी प्रांगण में ले जाकर वहाँ के पेड़ पौधे को दिखाकर पाठ पढ़ाते।

5. ग्राम पंचायत की कार्य–प्रणाली समझाने के लिए अध्यापक श्री रमेश चन्द्र छात्रों को ग्राम पंचायत की कार्यवाही में ले जाते हैं। अध्यापक का यह कार्य :

   (i) समय और श्रम की बर्बादी है।

   (ii) छात्रों का ज्ञान बढ़ाने में सहायक है।

   (iii) इससे गॉव वाले समझेंगे कि अध्यापक गांव के कार्यों में अनावश्यक हस्तक्षेप कर रहे हैं।

6. अध्यापक श्री अख्तर खान पुस्तक मेले से बच्चों के लिए उपयोगी पुस्तकें खरीदना चाहते हैं लेकिन धन की कमी के कारण स्वंय सभी पुस्तकें नहीं खरीद सकते। इसके लिए वे एक नया रास्ता अपनाते हैं, और सभी बच्चों से दो–दो रूपये स्वैच्छिक सहायता लेते हैं और पुस्तकें खरीदते हैं। आप इसे क्या मानेंगे –

   (i) छात्रों से इस तरह धन इकट्ठा करना अनुचित है।

   (ii) यदि पुस्तकें अत्यन्त छात्रोपयोगी हैं तो ऐसा किया जा सकता है।

   (iii) इस प्रकार पुस्तकें खरीदने से उन्हें सुरक्षित रखने का अनावश्यक बोझ बढ़ेगा।

7. पल्स पोलियो टीकाकरण अभियान के तहत शिक्षकों को यह कार्य दिया गया कि वे लोगों को इस विषय में जागरूक करें।

अध्यापक श्री शर्मा ने अपने कुछ छात्रों से इस विषय पर एक छोटे से नाटक का मंचन करवाया व गॉव के लोगों को इसमें आमंत्रित किया। आपकी दृष्टि में शिक्षक द्वारा किया गया यह कार्य –

(i) सराहनीय प्रयास है।

(ii) छात्रों को इस प्रकार के कार्य में लगाना उचित नहीं है।

(iii) अध्यापक को अतिरिक्त शैक्षिक कार्य को इतना महत्व नहीं देना चाहिए।

8. अध्यापक श्री जकाउल्ला खॉ इस बात से परेशान थे कि कुछ छात्र नियमित रूप से विद्यालय नहीं आ रहे हैं। अध्यापक ने सभी छात्रों से कहा कि अब उन्हें अपनी अनुपस्थिति का कारण अन्य सहपाठियों के समक्ष बताना पड़ेगा। यदि अध्यापक स्वंय भी अनुपस्थित रहते हैं तो उन्हें भी छात्रों को अनुपस्थिति का कारण बताना होगा। अध्यापक द्वारा निकाला गया समस्या का यह समाधान आपकी दृष्टि में –

(i) उचित है।

(ii) अध्यापक की छात्रों के प्रति कोई जबाबदेही नहीं होती

(iii) अध्यापक पद की गरिमा के अनुकूल कार्य नहीं है।

9. विद्यालय में प्रार्थना हो रही है। किसी छात्र का अभिभावक कुछ सूचना लेने विद्यालय में आता है। ऐसी परिस्थिति में आप क्या करेंगे ?

(i) अभिभावक से प्रतीक्षा करने का अनुरोध करूंगा।

(ii) अभिभावक से भी प्रार्थना में सम्मिलित होने का अनुरोध करूंगा।

(iii) अभिभावक को प्रार्थना सभा के बाद मिलने के लिए कहूंगा।

10. अध्यापिका कु0 इन्दिरा ने किसी कक्षा में एक नए प्रयोग द्वारा पढ़ाना शुरू किया। इस प्रयोग से उन्हें काफी सन्तुष्टि मिली और लगा कि बच्चों की उपलब्धि में सुधार हो रहा है। उनके इस भिन्न कार्य के सम्बन्ध में साथी अध्यापकों ने आलोचना आरम्भ कर दी। ऐसी स्थिति में आप हों तो क्या करेंगे?

(i) आप अपना प्रयोग बन्द कर देंगे और पुराने ढंग से पढ़ाने लगेंगे।

(ii) आप अपने साथी से सहयोग के लिए आग्रह करेंगे।

(iii) आप अपने साथी अध्यापकों की चर्चाओं पर ध्यान नहीं देंगे।

11. विद्यालय खुलने के समय आप विद्यालय आ जाते हैं परन्तु उस समय तक आपके प्रधानाध्यापक महोदय नहीं पहुँचे हैं। विद्यालय की चाभी उन्हीं के पास है। ऐसी स्थिति में यदि आप हों तो क्या करेंगे?

(i) विद्यालय के पास के किसी ग्रामीण के घर बैठ कर आप प्रधानाध्यापक की प्रतीक्षा करेंगे।

(ii) प्रधानाध्यापक के घर जाकर स्थिति ज्ञात करके चाभी लाकर विद्यालय खोलेंगे।

(iii) अपने घर वापस लौट जाएंगे।

खण्ड – 3

निर्देश : सर्वाधिक सही विकल्प के कमांक पर सही का निशान (✔) लगाइए।

1. कक्षा 5 में व्याकरण शिक्षण के लिए निम्नलिखित में से सर्वाधिक प्रभावी विधि रहेगी।

(i) पाठ्य पुस्तक विधि

(ii) सूत्र विधि

(iii) आगमन–निगमन विधि

(iv) उपरोक्त में से कोई नहीं

2. कविता की प्रस्तावना प्रस्तुत करने के लिए आप किस ढ़ंग का प्रयोग करेंगे?

अ. कविता के शीर्षक का परिचय देकर

ब. पाठ्य कविता की पृष्ठभूमि देते हुए

स. समभावी कविता की पंक्तियां प्रस्तुत करके

द. कविता का सस्वर पाठ करके

उत्तर– (i) अ और द (ii) केवल द (iii) ब, स और द (iv) अ, ब और स

3. छोटे बच्चों मैं मौखिक अभिव्यक्ति कौशल का विकास करने के लिए मै करूँगा –

   अ. औपचारिक बातचीत

   ब. व्याख्या

   स. अभिनय

   द. घटना वर्णन

उत्तर– (i) अ, ब और स (ii) अ, ब और द (iii) अ, स और द (iv) अ, ब, स और द

4. To teach meaning of any English word to the students of class IV, I will:

   (i) Give its meaning in Hindi

   (ii) Use flash cards

   (iii) Use pictures

   (iv) Explain it in simple English.

5. To encourage and promote good handwriting among the students I will:

   (i) Write on the black board and ask students to copy it.

   (ii) Encourage students to work in pairs.

   (iii) Encourage free writing and then check it.

   (iv) Request parents to supervise their handwriting at home.

6. To develop interest among my students towards English language I will :

   (i) Teach English language everyday in class.

   (ii) Tell them stories in English.

   (iii) Give them pictorial story books in English .. read by themselves

   (iv) Converse with them in English.

7. संस्कृत भाषा के शिक्षण में निम्न में से किस कौशल पर सर्वाधिक बल दिया जाना चाहिये।

(i) साहित्यिक सौन्दर्य का बोध

(ii) अर्थ बोध

(iii) नैतिक मूल्यों का बोध

(iv) मानसिक एवं भावात्मक बोध

8. संस्कृत भाषा के प्रति रूचि जागृत करने के लिए निम्न में से सबसे अधिक प्रभावी है –

(i) श्लोकों का सस्वर वाचन

(ii) व्याकरण के सूत्रों का ज्ञान

(iii) संस्कृत में निबंध लिखना

(iv) संस्कृत को संस्कृत माध्यम से पढ़ाना

9. 'ऊष्मा देने पर हवा फैलती है' इस तथ्य को समझाने का सर्वश्रेष्ठ तरीका है।

(i) व्याख्यान द्वारा

(ii) श्यामपट्ट पर चित्र बनाकर

(iii) एक फूले हुये गुब्बारे को ऊष्मा देकर

(iv) किसी बर्तन को गर्म करके।

10. आप विद्यार्थियों को किस तरह समझायेंगे कि बाहर छोड़ी हुई श्वास में ज्यादा आर्द्रता होती है?

(i) बाहर छोड़ी श्वास तथा अन्दर ली हुई श्वास के विभिन्न घटकों के प्रतिशत की तुलनात्मक तालिका बनाकर

(ii) शीशे के सामने श्वास छोड़कर

(iii) मौखिक रूप से व्याख्या करके

(iv) चार्ट द्वारा

11. पुष्प के विभिन्न भागों को समझाने के लिए आप क्या करेंगे?

(i) श्यामपट्ट पर चित्र बनायेंगे

(ii) पुष्प का माडल दिखायेंगे

(iii) पुष्प द्वारा समझाने का प्रयास करेंगे

(iv) उदाहरणों द्वारा समझायेंगे

12. प्राइमरी स्तर पर स्वच्छता की आदतों का विकास किस पर आधारित होना चाहिए?

(i) मौखिक व्याख्या पर

(ii) अभ्यास पर

(iii) चित्रों पर

(iv) उदाहरण प्रस्तुत करके

13. पानी में घुलनशीलता को आप किस तरह स्पष्ट करेंगे ?

(i) दो घुलनशील पदार्थ लेकर

(ii) दो अघुलनशील पदार्थ लेकर

(iii) एक घुलनशील और एक अघुलनशील पदार्थ लेकर

(iv) व्याख्या प्रस्तुत करके।

14. अपने विद्यार्थियों में वैज्ञानिक अभिवृत्ति के विकास हेतु आप क्या करेंगे?

(i) उन्हें टीकाकरण केन्द्र पर ले जाकर साधारण रोगों के बारे में समझाएंगे

(ii) उन्हें अपना वातावरण स्वच्छ रखना सिखाएंगे

(iii) विद्यार्थियों को पर्यावरण जागरूकता कार्यक्रमों में सहभागिता के लिए प्रोत्साहित करेंगे

(iv) उपरोक्त सभी

15. $1 + [1 \div 1 + \{ 1 - (1 + 1) \}] = ?$ को हल करने में कोष्ठकों का सही क्रम होगा –

(i) बड़ा कोष्ठक –– छोटा कोष्ठक –– मॅझला कोष्ठक

(ii) मॅझला कोष्ठक –– छोटा कोष्ठक –– बड़ा कोष्ठक

(iii) छोटा कोष्ठक –– मॅझला कोष्ठक –– बड़ा कोष्ठक

(iv) उपरोक्त में से कोई नहीं

16. 5/6 + 7/8 + 6/7 का योग छात्रों को सिखाने के लिए निम्नलिखित में से किसकी जानकारी आवश्यक है?

    (i) लघुत्तम समापवर्तक

    (ii) महत्तम समापवर्तक

    (iii) उपरोक्त दोनों

    (iv) दोनों में से कोई नहीं

17. कक्षा में 'भार' पढ़ाने के लिए आप निम्नलिखित में से कौन सी रणनीति अपनाएंगे ?

    (i) सभी प्रकार के भारों (बॅाटों) को कक्षा में लाकर छात्रों को दिखाएंगे

    (ii) दफ्ती के टुकड़ों पर बॅाटों का नाम लिखकर दिखायेंगे

    (iii) छात्रों को किसी दुकान में ले जाकर तुला और बाटों का प्रयोग दिखाएंगे।

    (iv) भार पढ़ाने के लिए भौतिक विज्ञान विषय से विशेष सहायक सामग्री ली जायेगी।

18. कक्षा–2 के छात्रों को घनाकार वस्तुओं के बारे में आप किस प्रकार पढ़ाएगें ?

    (i) कक्षा में घनाकर वस्तुओं के चित्र दिखाकर

    (ii) उपलब्ध घनाकार वस्तुएं दिखाकर

    (iii) छात्रों से स्वयं घनाकार वस्तुएं लाने को कहेंगे

    (iv) घनाकार वस्तुओं का मॉडल बनाकर

19. त्रिभुजों को वर्गीकृत कर सकते हैं ––

    (i) भुजाओं के आधार पर

    (ii) कोणों के आधार पर

    (iii) उपरोक्त दोनों के आधार पर

    (iv) क्षेत्रफल के आधार पर

20. किसी प्रश्न का उत्तर 512 घन मी0 है, निम्नलिखित में से यह हो सकता है–

(i) किसी आयत/वर्ग का क्षेत्रफल

(ii) किसी घन/घनाभ का आयतन

(iii) किसी बर्तन की धारिता

(iv) उपरोक्त में से कोई नहीं

21. इतिहास विषय की एक इकाई पढ़ाने के लिए अच्छा होगा कि –

(i) केवल ऐतिहासिक तथ्यों को ध्यान में रखा जाए

(ii) ऐतिहासिक, भौगोलिक, सामाजिक तथा अन्य महत्वपूर्ण तथ्यों को ध्यान में रखकर समग्र रूप से पढ़ाया जाए

(iii) इतिहास केवल भूतकाल की घटनाओं के रूप में पढ़ाया जाए

(iv) इतिहास को वास्तविक जीवन से जोड़कर पढ़ाया जाए

22. कक्षा 4 के विद्यार्थियों को भारत के मानचित्र की सहायता से भौगोलिक दशाओं का ज्ञान देने हेतु आप क्या करेगें ?

(i) विद्यार्थियों के लिए मानचित्र बनाकर उसमें पर्वत एवं नदियां दर्शाने को कहेंगे

(ii) बने बनाये मानचित्र पर स्वयं नदियां तथा पर्वत दर्शायेगे

(iii) यामपट्ट पर भारत का मानचित्र बनाकर किसी विद्यार्थी को बुलाकर नदियां एवं पर्वत दर्शाने के लिए कहेगे

(iv) केवल पाठ्यपुस्तक के माध्यम से पढ़ायेंगे

23. पर्यावरण प्रदूषण की जानकारी देने के लिए आप क्या करेगे ?

(i) पुस्तक में दिया गया पाठ पढ़ायेंगे

(ii) प्रदूषण से सम्बंधित चार्ट दिखायेंगे

(iii) बच्चों को आस–पास के क्षेत्र का भ्रमण कराते हुए मार्ग में पड़ने वाले प्रदूषण जनित स्थानों को दिखाकर उनके दुष्प्रभावों से अवगत करायेंगे।

(iv) पर्यावरण प्रदूषण पर एक फिल्म दिखायेंगे

24. आपकी कक्षा के एक छात्र को चॉक खाने की बुरी आदत है। उसकी इस आदत को छुड़ाने के लिए आप क्या करेंगे–

(i) बच्चे को डांटेंगे

(ii) उसे चॉक खाने से होने वाले नुकसान के बारे में बतायेंगे

(iii) सम्पूर्ण कक्षा को भोजन एवं उत्तम स्वास्थ्य हेतु अच्छी आदतें विकसित करने के लिए प्रेरित करेंगे

(iv) बच्चे के अभिभावक को बुलाकर उसकी बुरी आदत के बारे में बतायेंगे

25. बच्चों में अच्छी नागरिकता के गुण विकसित करने हेतु–

(i) गांव के सम्भ्रांत नागरिकों से छात्रों की बातचीत करायेंगे

(ii) अच्छे नागरिक के गुणों के बारे में बतायेंगे

(iii) शिक्षक अपने दिन प्रतिदिन के सद्आचरण के द्वारा छात्रों को प्रेरित करेंगे

(iv) देश के श्रेष्ठ नागरिकों के बारे में जानकारी देंगे

26. सामाजिक विषय के मूल्यांकन हेतु आप संर्वाधिक महत्वपूर्ण समझते हैं —

(i) तथ्यों के प्रमाणिकता एवं सत्यता को

(ii) लेखन सामग्री की मात्रा को

(iii) भाषा प्रवाह को

(iv) तार्किक दृष्टिकोण को

खण्ड – 4

निर्देश : प्रश्न सं. 1 के स्तम्भ I में क, ख, ग एवं घ दिए हुए हैं जिन्हें स्तम्भ II में दिए गए विकल्पों i. ii. iii. व iv से सुमेलित करना है।

1. **स्तम्भ I** — **स्तम्भ II**

स्तम्भ I	स्तम्भ II
क. संस्मरण	(i) अपनी जीवन कथा का आत्मीयता से प्रस्तुतीकरण
ख. जीवनी	(ii) किसी घटना का यथातथ्य एवं सजीव प्रस्तुतीकरण

ग. आत्मकथा	(iii) किसी वस्तु, व्यक्ति या घटना सम्बन्धी आधारित विवरण
घ. रिपोर्ताज	(iv) किसी महापुरूष या प्रसिद्ध व्यक्ति की जीवन कथा का आत्मीयतापूर्ण वर्णन

2. यहाँ कुछ पंक्तियां दी जा रही हैं। प्रत्येक पंक्ति का विस्तार करके कविता पूरी कीजिए।

सूरज के संग आती धूप, ...

जाड़े में मन भाती धूप, ...

सुन्दर फूल खिलाती धूप, ...

कपड़े रोज सुखाती धूप, ...

निर्देश : प्रश्न सं0 3 और 4 में सर्वाधिक सही विकल्प के कमांक पर सही (✓)का निशान लगाएं।

3. जिस रचना में वर्ण, मात्रा यति, गति, तुक आदि का ज्ञान रखा जाता है उसे कहते हैं।

(i) सवैया

(ii) छन्द

(iii) दोहा

(iv) उपर्युक्त में से कोई नहीं

4. फूल से हमें क्या सीख मिलती है ?

(i) हमें ओस और कांटों के बीच भी खिलना चाहिए।

(ii) हमें सर्दी गर्मी, बरसात की परवाह नहीं करनी चाहिए।

(iii) हमें दुःख के क्षणों व कठिनाइयों में भी प्रसन्न रहना चाहिए।

(iv) हमें फूलों की तरह महकना चाहिए।

5. निम्नलिखित दो वाक्यों में उचित विराम चिन्हों का प्रयोग कीजिये।

(i) ओह पिछली रात मुझे बाहर जाना पड़ा

(ii) राधा ने झुर्रियों से भरे चेहरे की ओर देखा और बोली आपका परिवार कहाँ है

6. निम्नलिखित में से प्रत्येक वाक्यों हेतु एक शब्द लिखिए।

(i) साहस से युक्त व्यक्ति ________________

(ii) भवन योजना बनाने वाला ________________

(iii) कम व्यय करने वाला ________________

(iv) भगवान में न विश्वास करने वाला ________________

7. नीचे लिखे शब्दों के तत्सम रूप लिखिए।

(i) बरस ....

(ii) धरम ....

(iii) दीया ....

(iv) करम ....

8- Use ' in ', 'on' or 'at' with the following:

______the field ______the playground

______the swing ______the river bank

______the platform ______the chair

______the sofa ______the well

9. Give opposites of the following:

(i) Young ....

(ii) Strong ....

(iii) Ugly ....

(iv) Straight ....

10. Translate the following sentences in English:

(i) कोयल और तितलियाँ बगीचे में उड़ रही हैं। ....

(ii) मगरमच्छ नदी में तैर रहा है। ....

(iii) हाथी की एक लम्बी सूड़ होती है। ....

(iv) मेरा कंघा यहाँ है। ....

11. Answer the following questions:

(i) Where is the apple? Ans. ....

(ii) Where is the rabbit? Ans. ....

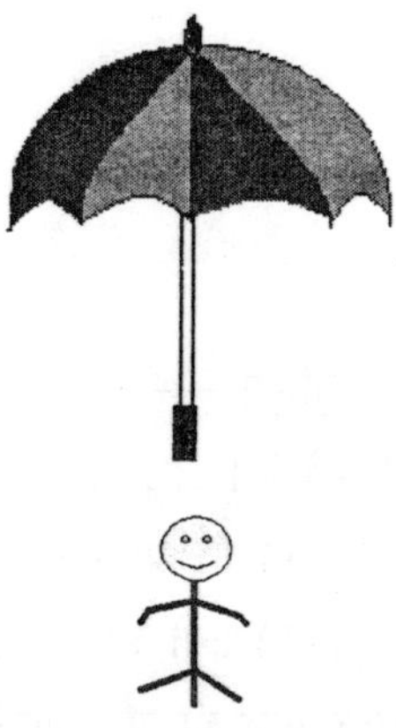

(iii) Where is the boy standing? Ans. ....

(iv) Where is the bus ? Ans. ....

निर्देश : सर्वाधिक सही विकल्प के कमांक पर सही (✓) का निशान लगाइए।

12. संस्कृत व्याकरण के सम्बन्ध में निम्न में से कौन से कथन सत्य हैं।

(क) वचन– एकवचन और बहुवचन होते हैं ।

(ख) पुरूष – प्रथम, मध्यम और उत्तम पुरूष होते हैं।

(ग) लिंग – पुल्लिंग, स्त्रीलिंग होते हैं।

(घ) संधियां – स्वर संधि, गुण संधि होती हैं।

उत्तर– (i) क और ग (ii) ख और ग

(iii) क,ख और ग (iv) क,ख,ग और घ

13. स्तम्भ I तथा स्तम्भ II की प्रविष्टियों को सुमेलित कीजिए।

स्तम्भ I	स्तम्भ II
(क) नादं	(1) आवश्यकता
(ख) नीडम्	(2) घोसला
(ग) आनय	(3) हाथ जोड़कर
(घ) सांजलि	(4) ले जाना
	(5) ाब्द को

14. संस्कृत में अनुवाद कीजिए —

(i) पत्ते पेड़ से गिरते हैं। ....

(ii) राम ने रावण पर विजय प्राप्त की। ....

(iii) क्रोध दुर्बलता की निशानी होता है। ....

(iv) भारत का अतीत बड़ा ही गौरवशाली रहा है। ....

निर्देश : सर्वाधिक सही उत्तर के कमांक पर सही (✓) का निशान लगाइये।

15. निम्न लिखित में से कौन तना नहीं है?

(i) आलू (ii) अदरख

(iii) शलजम (iv) हल्दी

16. मेंढक जल तथा थल दोनों में रह सकता है क्योंकि :

(i) पैरों की उंगलियों में जाल होते हैं

(ii) सांस लेने के लिये फेफड़े होते हैं

(iii) त्वचा में नमी होती है

(iv) उपरोक्त सभी

17. पृथ्वी से चन्द्रमा किस स्थिति में नहीं दिखाई पड़ता?

(i) सूर्य ग्रहण में

(ii) चन्द्र ग्रहण में

(iii) दोनों स्थितियों में

(iv) दोनों स्थितियों में नहीं

18. निम्नलिखित में से किस स्थिति में कार्य हो रहा है?

(i) एक व्यक्ति कमरे की दीवार पर बल लगा रहा है

(ii) एक बच्चा चलते हुए खिलौने को रोकने का प्रयास कर रहा है

(iii) इंजन द्वारा ट्रेन खींचा जा रहा है

(iv) उपरोक्त सभी स्थितियों में

निर्देश : प्रश्न संख्या 19 एवं 20 के कथनों के सामने सही (✓) या गलत (x) का चिन्ह लगाइये।

19. (i) नागफनी एक मरूस्थलीय पौधा है। ( )

(ii) पक्षियों के मुँह में दांत पाये जाते हैं। ( )

(iii) जलीय पौधों के तने कोमल एवं हल्के होते हैं। ( )

(iv) हृदय द्वारा रक्त छानने का कार्य होता है। ( )

20. (i) तूतिया जल में अविलेय है। ( )

(ii) मोम मिट्टी के तेल में विलेय है। ( )

(iii) बालू पेट्रोल में विलेय है। ( )

(iv) तारकोल पेट्रोल में विलेय है। ( )

21. स्तम्भ I की प्रविष्टियों को स्तम्भ II की प्रविष्टियों से सुमेलित कीजिए :

स्तम्भ I	स्तम्भ II
(i) कब्जा संधि	अ) घुटना
(ii) गेंद– गड्ढा संधि	ब) कन्धा
(iii) पेशियां	स) गति
(iv) मेरूदण्ड	द) रीढ़
	य) उंगली

22. निम्नलिखित चित्र में पुष्प के भागों के नाम लिखिए:

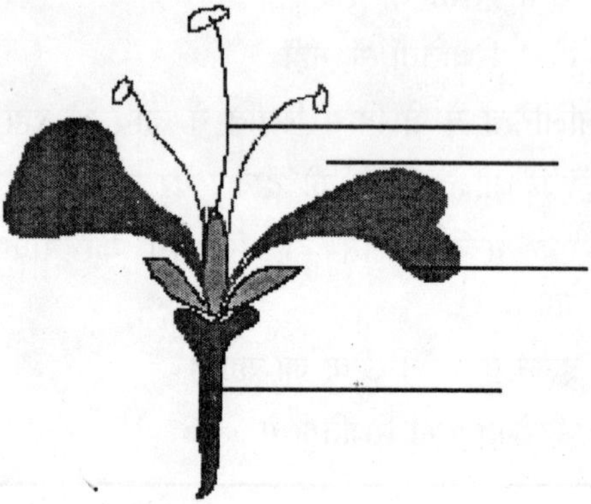

> **निर्देश : इस भाग में दिए गए प्रश्नों (23 से 28) के कई विकल्प उत्तर दिए गए हैं। विकल्पों में से सर्वाधिक सही उत्तर के कमांक पर सही (✓) का निशान लगाइये।**

23. 2.5 , 2.05 तथा 0.205 का योग होगा ––

(i) 0.4755 (ii) 47.55

(iii) 4.755 (iv) 2.755

24. दो संख्याओं का गुणनफल 60 है। यदि उनमें से एक संख्या गुणनफल हो, तो दूसरी संख्या होगी–

(i) 60 (ii) 0

(iii) 1 (iv) दिये गए ऑकड़े अपर्याप्त हैं ।

25. यदि वर्ग की एक भुजा की लम्बाई तीन गुनी कर दी जाय तो वर्ग का क्षेत्रफल हो जाएगा –

(i) तीन गुना (ii) नौ गुना

(iii) चार गुना (iv) कोई अन्तर नहीं पड़ेगा

26. दो संख्याओं का लघुत्तम समापवर्तक तथा महत्तम समापवर्तक क्रमश : 100 तथा 40 है। यदि एक संख्या 200 है, तो दूसरी संख्या क्या होगी ?

(i) 80 (ii) 50

(iii) 60 (iv) 40

27. दस आदमी एक काम को 30 दिन में कर लेते हैं। उसी काम को 25 दिन में पूरा करने में कितने आदमियों की आवश्यकता होगी ?

(i) 36 (ii) 8

(iii) 12 (iv) 16

28. एक व्यक्ति 1 किमी0 चलने के बाद 1/2 किमी0 पीछे लौट आता है। 8 किमी0 की दूरी तय करने में उसे कुल कितने किमी0 चलना होगा ?

(i) 21 किमी0 (ii) 22 किमी0

(iii) 16 किमी0 (iv) 40 किमी0

29. 1 किमी0 में सेमी0 होंगे..

30. 60 के 20 प्रतिशत का 60 प्रतिशत होगा ....

निर्देशः सर्वाधिक सही उत्तर के कमांक पर सही (✓) का निशान लगाएं।

31. निम्नलिखित में से गांव पंचायत के कार्य कहे जाएंगे –

अ. गांव में सफाई की व्यवस्था करना।

ब. शिक्षा की व्यवस्था की देख–रेख करना।

स. चिकित्सीय सुविधाओं का ध्यान रखना।

द. राजस्व की वसूली करना।

(i) अ ब स द (ii) ब द अ

(iii) अ ब स (iv) ब स द

32. निम्नलिखित में से कौन सा कथन सही नहीं है ?

(i) हर प्रदेश में एक विधानसभा होती है।

(ii) हर प्रदेश में एक विधानसभा और एक विधानपरिषद होती है।

(iii) विधान परिषद के सदस्य को एम0एल0सी0 कहा जाता है।

(iv) विधानसभा के अध्यक्ष का चुनाव विधानसभा के सदस्यों में से होता है।

33. जहांगीर कालीन स्थापत्य की प्रमुख विशेषता थी –

(i) गुम्बद (ii) मीनार

(iii) लाल पत्थर (iv) सफेद संगमरमर

34. निम्न में से कौन सा कथन धर्म के अर्थ को स्पष्ट करता है–

(i) धार्मिक व्यक्ति का निर्माण करना।

(ii) जीवन–दर्शन प्राप्त करने में सहायता देना।

(iii) निर्वाण–प्राप्ति का मार्ग प्रशस्त करना।

(iv) मनुष्य को नैतिक बनाने में सहायक होना।

35. निम्न में से 'असत्य' कथन को पहचानिये –

(i) चीनी भाषा ऊपर से नीचे लिखी जाती है।

(ii) अफगानिस्तान की मुख्य भाषा पश्तो है।

(iii) चंदन, शीशम, बरगद तथा पीपल सदाबहार वन के उदाहरण हैं।

(iv) मकर रेखा और कर्क रेखा के बीच में भूमध्य रेखा है।

36. दक्षिण पश्चिमी मानसून कहते हैं –

(i) बंगाल की खाड़ी से उठने वाले मानसूनों को।

(ii) अरब सागर से उठने वाले मानसूनों को।

(iii) हिन्द महासागर से उठने वाले मानसूनें को।

(iv) अटलांटिक महासागर से उठने वाले मानसूनो को।

37. 'विजयी विश्व तिरंगा प्यारा' गीत किसने लिखा है–

(i) श्यामलाल गुप्त (ii) महात्मा गांधी

(iii) बंकिम चन्द्र चटर्जी (iv) रवीन्द्रनाथ टैगोर

38. निम्नलिखित में से प्रदूषण बढ़ाने में कौन सा कारक उत्तरदायी नहीं है –

(i) झूम खेती (ii) बड़े–बड़े बांधों का निर्माण

(iii) मौती प्रथा (iv) कागज के कारखाने

खण्ड – 5

1. राष्ट्रीय ध्वज का चित्र बनाइए।

2. चित्र 'ब' चित्र 'अ' की नकल है, परन्तु चित्र 'ब' में पाँच त्रुटियां हैं। उन्हें छाँटकर लिखिए।

अ

ब

1. 2. 3. 4. 5.

3. अपने विद्यालय की प्रत्येक कक्षा के विद्यार्थियों की संख्या बताते हुए उन्हें वृत्त चित्र (पाई डायग्राम) में दर्शाइए।

कक्षा	विद्यार्थी संख्या	वृत्त चित्र
1	....	
2	....	
3	....	
4	....	
5	....	

4. पुल, रेल लाइन तथा विद्यालय को संकेत चिन्हों के द्वारा दिखाइए।

पुल		रेल लाइन		विद्यालय

5. चार विद्यालयों अ, ब, स, तथा द में विद्यार्थियों की संख्या कमशः 110, 125, 100 तथा 90 हैं। इसे दण्ड चित्र द्वारा दर्शाइए।

6. आम, मोमबत्ती तथा बक्से के चित्र बनाइए।

7. चार लाइन कापी के अनुसार निम्न वाक्य को अंग्रेजी के छोटे अक्षरों में लिखिए।

THE QUICK BROWN FOX JUMPS RIGHT OVER THE LAZY DOG

....

....

....

....

....

....

....

....

8. चित्र बनाकर निम्नांकित में अन्तर स्पष्ट करें।

1. घन और घनाभ

2. आयत और समानान्तर चतुर्भुज

9. एक विद्यार्थी घर से विद्यालय की ओर चला। वह पहले 100 मीटर उत्तर की ओर चला फिर वह 25 मीटर पश्चिम की ओर चला, उसके पश्चात वह 40 मीटर सीधे दक्षिण की ओर चला। एक अनुमानित मापक लेकर इसे चित्र के माध्यम से दर्शाए ।

10. एक विद्यार्थी कविता का सस्वर वाचन कर रहा है। उसका मूल्यांकन करने में आप किन–किन बारीकियों का ध्यान रखेंगे?

11. भारत का मानचित्र बनाइए।

Appendix-B

Data Collected on Primary School Teachers

(N=200)

	Teaching Competencies Scores						Variables					
SN	**TC-1**	**TC-2**	**TC-3**	**TC-4**	**TC-5**	**Total**	**Qualification**	**Training**	**Discipline**	**Experience**	**Gender**	**Habitant**
1	48	9	18	25	0	100	PG	BTC	Arts	< 10	Male	Rural
2	38	9	16	33	7	103	PG	VBTC	Science	< 10	Male	Rural
3	41	0	14	27	12	94	Inter	BTC	Arts	> 20	Male	Rural
4	46	4	16	29	5	100	G	VBTC	Arts	< 10	Male	Rural
5	52	7	10	41	16	126	G	VBTC	Science	< 10	Male	Rural
6	46	4	16	29	5	100	HS	BTC	Science	> 20	Male	Rural
7	60	7	21	40	22	150	PG	VBTC	Science	< 10	Male	Rural
8	60	8	14	0	0	82	PG	VBTC	Science	< 10	Male	Rural
9	48	10	16	22	14	110	Inter	BTC	Science	10 _20	Male	Rural
10	50	6	19	32	10	117	Inter	BTC	Arts	< 10	Male	Rural
11	53	7	19	37	15	131	PG	BTC	Arts	< 10	Female	Rural
12	52	7	14	35	11	119	HS	BTC	Arts	> 20	Female	Rural
13	42	8	11	28	15	104	Inter	B.Ed	Arts	< 10	Female	Rural
14	47	7	8	35	0	97	Inter	BTC	Arts	< 10	Female	Rural

15	52	9	12	34	6	113	Inter	BTC	Arts	> 20	Male	Rural
16	37	6	7	2	0	52	Inter	BTC	Arts	< 10	Female	Rural
17	46	4	15	38	8	111	Inter	BTC	Science	< 10	Male	Rural
18	40	7	7	33	30	117	Inter	BTC	Arts	10_20	Male	Rural
19	44	8	12	37	5	106	G	BTC	Arts	10_20	Female	Rural
20	52	9	15	38	16	130	G	BTC	Arts	10_20	Female	Rural
21	37	3	6	9	1	56	G	VBTC	Science	< 10	Male	Rural
22	52	8	12	34	8	114	G	BTC	Arts	10_20	Female	Rural
23	35	7	1	0	1	44	G	B.Ed	Arts	< 10	Female	Rural
24	45	7	14	30	10	106	HS	BTC	Arts	> 20	Male	Rural
25	30	7	7	27	7	78	HS	BTC	Arts	> 20	Male	Rural
26	51	5	18	42	12	128	Inter	BTC	Arts	> 20	Male	Rural
27	39	7	15	41	15	117	HS	BTC	Arts	> 20	Male	Rural
28	47	7	20	13	14	101	Inter	BTC	Commerce	< 10	Male	Rural
29	37	10	14	40	11	112	HS	JBT	Arts	> 20	Female	Rural
30	47	6	13	29	15	110	Inter	BTC	Science	> 20	Male	Rural
31	49	7	5	30	12	103	Inter	BTC	Arts	> 20	Male	Rural
32	45	5	15	27	9	101	G	BTC	Arts	< 10	Female	Rural
33	57	8	15	18	2	100	PG	VBTC	Science	< 10	Male	Rural

34	51	9	15	39	12	126	G	B.Ed	Science	< 10	Male	Rural
35	44	5	10	8	8	75	HS	BTC	Commerce	> 20	Male	Rural
36	44	5	9	39	15	112	PG	B.Ed	Arts	< 10	Female	Rural
37	50	9	17	41	9	126	PG	VBTC	Arts	< 10	Male	Rural
38	49	5	14	29	10	107	G	BTC	Arts	10_20	Male	Rural
39	43	0	5	31	7	86	Inter	BTC	Arts	< 10	Female	Rural
40	53	8	19	38	10	128	G	BTC	Science	< 10	Male	Rural
41	52	7	19	24	3	105	G	VBTC	Arts	< 10	Male	Rural
42	49	6	14	27	10	106	Inter	BTC	Arts	< 10	Female	Rural
43	48	8	15	37	9	117	G	BTC	Commerce	10_20	Male	Rural
44	44	8	22	18	5	127	G	VBTC	Science	< 10	Female	Rural
45	45	9	11	28	10	103	HS	BTC	Commerce	> 20	Male	Rural
46	52	7	13	20	0	92	PG	VBTC	Science	< 10	Female	Rural
47	58	9	17	29	8	121	Inter	BTC	Arts	10_20	Female	Rural
48	53	10	17	31	9	120	G	BTC	Science	< 10	Male	Rural
49	43	10	16	41	14	124	G	BTC	Science	10_20	Female	Rural
50	38	0	0	10	4	52	HS	BTC	Commerce	> 20	Male	Rural
51	55	10	18	35	26	144	G	BTC	Arts	< 10	Female	Rural

52	51	7	14	39	22	133	Inter	BTC	Arts	10_20	Male	Rural
53	53	10	18	37	28	146	Inter	JBT	Science	> 20	Male	Rural
54	43	10	11	32	11	107	PG	VBTC	Arts	< 10	Female	Rural
55	51	8	10	19	3	91	G	BTC	Science	< 10	Female	Rural
56	63	9	18	41	27	158	PG	VBTC	Arts	< 10	Female	Rural
57	47	8	10	21	0	86	G	BTC	Arts	< 10	Female	Rural
58	51	10	16	44	20	141	PG	BTC	Science	< 10	Female	Rural
59	61	9	19	46	26	161	G	VBTC	Science	< 10	Female	Rural
60	61	9	18	48	28	164	PG	JBT	Arts	> 20	Male	Rural
61	55	9	19	46	23	152	Inter	BTC	Science	10_20	Male	Rural
62	60	9	19	49	26	163	PG	VBTC	Science	< 10	Female	Rural
63	51	9	17	50	28	155	Inter	BTC	Science	< 10	Male	Rural
64	60	9	18	50	25	162	G	BTC	Commerce	< 10	Female	Rural
65	60	9	20	46	25	160	PG	BTC	Science	< 10	Male	Rural
66	14	4	10	35	3	66	Inter	BTC	Arts	> 20	Male	Rural
67	45	2	6	12	5	70	G	BTC	Arts	> 20	Male	Rural
68	45	0	4	30	1	80	HS	JBT	Science	> 20	Male	Rural
69	59	9	19	50	31	168	PG	VBTC	Arts	< 10	Male	Rural
70	57	1	16	28	6	108	PG	VBTC	Science	< 10	Male	Rural

71	60	7	20	46	10	143	PG	BTC	Science	< 10	Female	Rural
72	47	4	11	16	0	78	HS	BTC	Arts	> 20	Male	Rural
73	34	8	17	45	20	124	G	BTC	Arts	< 10	Female	Rural
74	46	7	18	3	13	87	BTC	BTC	Arts	< 10	Female	Rural
75	56	7	16	26	6	111	PG	VBTC	Arts	< 10	Female	Rural
76	59	8	9	30	10	116	PG	BTC	Science	< 10	Female	Rural
77	45	4	11	9	3	72	PG	BTC	Arts	< 10	Male	Rural
78	56	7	16	42	17	138	G	VBTC	Science	< 10	Female	Rural
79	59	8	16	41	10	134	PG	VBTC	Arts	< 10	Female	Rural
80	34	8	17	38	8	105	G	BTC	Arts	< 10	Female	Rural
81	54	8	15	34	5	116	PG	VBTC	Arts	< 10	Male	Rural
82	42	9	14	7	0	72	G	BTC	Arts	< 10	Male	Rural
83	39	7	2	1	0	49	G	VBTC	Arts	< 10	Female	Rural
84	45	7	11	22	0	85	Inter	BTC	Arts	< 10	Female	Rural
85	51	7	8	17	0	83	G	BTC	Arts	> 20	Male	Rural
86	40	9	6	11	1	67	Inter	BTC	Arts	< 10	Female	Rural
87	38	10	13	8	4	73	G	VBTC	Arts	< 10	Female	Rural
88	50	9	11	29	5	104	G	BTC	Science	> 20	Male	Rural

89	30	6	6	0	0	42	PG	VBTC	Arts	< 10	Female	Rural
90	25	8	11	2	0	46	Inter	BTC	Arts	> 20	Male	Rural
91	32	7	10	34	6	89	G	VBTC	Arts	< 10	Male	Rural
92	48	8	11	30	4	101	G	BTC	Commerce	< 10	Male	Rural
93	52	6	11	13	0	82	G	BTC	Arts	> 20	Female	Rural
94	46	7	4	24	3	84	G	VBTC	Commerce	< 10	Male	Rural
95	56	6	19	40	7	128	G	VBTC	Arts	< 10	Male	Rural
96	48	7	14	30	18	117	G	VBTC	Science	< 10	Female	Rural
97	56	8	13	36	13	126	G	VBTC	Arts	< 10	Male	Rural
98	45	4	8	18	18	93	Inter	BTC	Arts	10_20	Female	Rural
99	63	8	18	35	26	150	PG	VBTC	Arts	< 10	Male	Rural
100	46	6	17	34	12	115	G	BTC	Arts	< 10	Male	Rural
101	36	7	16	41	15	115	Inter	BTC	Arts	> 20	Female	Urban
102	50	8	12	4	0	74	Inter	BTC	Arts	> 20	Female	Urban
103	49	6	16	41	14	126	G	BTC	Arts	> 20	Female	Urban
104	43	9	18	42	10	122	Inter	BTC	Arts	< 10	Male	Urban
105	54	9	21	46	21	151	PG	BTC	Arts	< 10	Female	Urban
106	54	9	21	45	19	148	G	BTC	Arts	< 10	Female	Urban
107	61	10	18	48	22	159	PG	BTC	Arts	< 10	Female	Urban

108	59	9	21	42	15	146	G	BTC	Science	10 _20	Female	Urban
109	44	8	17	44	17	130	HS	BTC	Science	10 _20	Female	Urban
110	41	0	7	10	2	60	G	BTC	Arts	10 _20	Female	Urban
111	52	5	11	37	25	130	PG	VBTC	Arts	> 20	Female	Urban
112	44	2	2	18	9	75	Inter	BTC	Arts	10 _20	Female	Urban
113	47	8	14	30	3	102	Inter	BTC	Arts	< 10	Female	Urban
114	42	7	13	28	12	102	HS	JBT	Science	> 20	Male	Urban
115	50	6	14	38	18	126	PG	BTC	Arts	10 _20	Female	Urban
116	51	7	9	22	7	96	G	BTC	Arts	> 20	Female	Urban
117	51	7	11	23	8	100	PG	BTC	Arts	> 20	Female	Urban
118	50	4	10	23	0	87	G	BTC	Arts	> 20	Female	Urban
119	43	5	13	22	15	98	Inter	BTC	Arts	< 10	Female	Urban
120	42	8	16	35	14	115	G	BTC	Arts	< 10	Female	Urban
121	50	10	17	26	8	111	G	BTC	Science	< 10	Male	Urban
122	60	9	19	32	18	138	PG	BTC	Arts	< 10	Female	Urban
123	52	7	15	22	18	114	G	BTC	Arts	< 10	Male	Urban
124	40	8	11	23	10	92	HS	JBT	Arts	> 20	Female	Urban
125	45	10	13	19	5	118	G	VBTC	Science	< 10	Female	Urban

126	50	10	13	28	9	110	G	BTC	Commerce	> 20	Male	Urban
127	51	6	14	27	10	108	Inter	BTC	Arts	< 10	Female	Urban
128	50	6	17	30	12	115	G	VBTC	Arts	< 10	Male	Urban
129	55	7	18	38	13	131	G	VBTC	Arts	< 10	Male	Urban
130	44	4	5	27	8	88	Inter	BTC	Arts	< 10	Female	Urban
131	54	9	19	41	14	137	PG	VBTC	Arts	< 10	Male	Urban
132	51	6	16	42	16	131	PG	BTC	Science	< 10	Female	Urban
133	42	4	8	10	7	71	HS	JBT	Arts	> 20	Male	Urban
134	52	10	17	40	14	133	G	BTC	Science	< 10	Female	Urban
135	58	8	19	40	19	144	PG	BTC	Science	10 _20	Male	Urban
136	44	4	11	20	7	86	G	BTC	Arts	< 10	Female	Urban
137	48	6	6	22	11	93	Inter	JBT	Arts	> 20	Male	Urban
138	46	5	11	24	14	100	Inter	JBT	Science	> 20	Male	Urban
139	36	9	11	34	15	105	HS	JBT	Arts	> 20	Male	Urban
140	48	8	19	20	14	109	Inter	BTC	Commerce	< 10	Female	Urban
141	38	6	15	36	13	108	HS	JBT	Arts	> 20	Male	Urban
142	52	6	18	41	13	130	Inter	JBT	Arts	> 20	Female	Urban
143	31	8	8	25	7	79	HS	JBT	Arts	> 20	Male	Urban
144	53	9	14	31	10	117	G	BTC	Arts	10 _20	Female	Urban

145	53	8	12	32	8	113	G	BTC	Arts	10_20	Female	Urban
146	38	6	13	30	12	99	G	VBTC	Science	< 10	Male	Urban
147	53	10	16	39	17	135	G	BTC	Arts	10_20	Female	Urban
148	44	8	14	36	11	113	G	BTC	Arts	10_20	Female	Urban
149	51	6	10	31	13	111	HS	JBT	Arts	> 20	Female	Urban
150	42	7	13	27	14	103	Inter	JBT	Science	> 20	Male	Urban
151	51	10	14	48	20	143	G	BTC	Arts	> 20	Female	Urban
152	48	7	14	47	26	142	Inter	BTC	Arts	> 20	Female	Urban
153	49	9	18	38	11	125	G	BTC	Arts	> 20	Male	Urban
154	51	5	16	37	23	132	PG	BTC	Arts	10_20	Male	Urban
155	56	8	23	48	29	164	G	BTC	Arts	< 10	Female	Urban
156	49	6	16	44	13	128	Inter	BTC	Arts	> 20	Male	Urban
157	49	8	20	42	29	148	G	BTC	Arts	10_20	Female	Urban
158	44	8	18	44	30	144	PG	BTC	Arts	10_20	Female	Urban
159	51	8	16	27	17	119	Inter	BTC	Science	> 20	Female	Urban
160	44	8	9	9	0	70	HS	JBT	Arts	> 20	Male	Urban
161	46	3	6	8	0	63	G	BTC	Arts	< 10	Female	Urban
162	31	8	12	37	13	101	Inter	JBT	Arts	> 20	Male	Urban

163	45	7	14	32	15	113	G	BTC	Arts	< 10	Female	Urban
164	64	9	19	36	25	153	PG	VBTC	Arts	< 10	Male	Urban
165	46	5	11	19	17	98	Inter	BTC	Arts	< 10	Female	Urban
166	55	8	14	31	18	126	G	VBTC	Science	< 10	Female	Urban
167	56	8	13	37	14	128	G	VBTC	Arts	< 10	Male	Urban
168	55	6	19	37	8	125	G	VBTC	Arts	< 10	Male	Urban
169	47	8	11	30	4	100	G	VBTC	Commerce	< 10	Male	Urban
170	53	7	16	17	5	98	G	BTC	Arts	> 20	Female	Urban
171	49	9	15	34	6	113	G	BTC	Arts	< 10	Male	Urban
172	40	8	16	32	7	103	G	VBTC	Arts	< 10	Male	Urban
173	26	9	14	15	11	75	Inter	BTC	Arts	> 20	Male	Urban
174	31	7	10	14	15	77	Inter	BTC	Science	> 20	Female	Urban
175	51	8	14	32	6	111	Inter	BTC	Science	> 20	Male	Urban
176	39	11	16	15	11	92	G	VBTC	Arts	< 10	Female	Urban
177	41	8	8	18	6	81	G	BTC	Arts	< 10	Female	Urban
178	52	8	8	24	4	96	G	BTC	Arts	> 20	Male	Urban
179	46	8	14	27	12	107	Inter	BTC	Arts	< 10	Female	Urban
180	40	8	6	12	5	71	G	BTC	Arts	< 10	Female	Urban
181	55	9	20	34	17	135	PG	BTC	Arts	< 10	Male	Urban

182	35	8	21	39	10	113	G	BTC	Arts	< 10	Female	Urban
183	60	7	20	43	16	146	PG	VBTC	Arts	< 10	Female	Urban
184	55	6	19	48	18	146	G	VBTC	Science	< 10	Female	Urban
185	46	5	14	22	15	102	PG	BTC	Arts	10_20	Male	Urban
186	60	10	16	35	15	136	PG	BTC	Science	10_20	Female	Urban
187	57	8	17	30	7	119	PG	VBTC	Arts	< 10	Female	Urban
188	47	8	16	39	15	125	G	BTC	Arts	< 10	Female	Urban
189	36	10	15	47	21	129	G	BTC	Arts	10_20	Female	Urban
190	49	6	14	23	5	97	HS	JBT	Arts	> 20	Male	Urban
191	61	8	25	46	14	154	PG	BTC	Science	< 10	Female	Urban
192	60	10	18	51	29	168	PG	VBTC	Arts	< 10	Male	Urban
193	21	4	6	18	6	55	HS	JBT	Science	> 20	Female	Urban
194	46	8	9	19	6	88	G	BTC	Arts	> 20	Male	Urban
195	62	10	20	44	21	157	PG	BTC	Science	< 10	Male	Urban
196	61	9	19	49	21	159	PG	BTC	Commerce	< 10	Female	Urban
197	60	10	17	47	23	157	PG	VBTC	Science	< 10	Female	Urban
198	53	8	19	43	23	146	PG	BTC	Arts	< 10	Female	Urban
199	62	8	15	33	19	137	PG	VBTC	Arts	< 10	Female	Urban
200	50	8	13	39	21	131	G	VBTC	Arts	< 10	Female	Urban

Bibliography

Anantha Krishnan, J. (1988). Who Go To Colleges of Education? - A Comprehensive Study of the Socio-Economic and Educational Background of Students of Selected B.Ed. Courses in Pune, 1986-87. In Buch, M.B. (Ed.), *Fifth Survey of Educational Research*. (1988-92), Vol. II, New Delhi : NCERT, p. 1207.

Acar, F. E. (2008). An assessment of Social Studies Competency of Turkish Classroom Teachers. *International Journal of Instruction.* From http:/www.doaj.org.

Anandan K. and Rajasekaram P. (2005). Relationship between Teaching Competency and Attitude towards Teaching Social Science among Distance Learners of B.Ed. *Journal of Community Guidance and Research,* 2005, Vol. 22, (2), Hyderabad : Neelkamal Publications Pvt. Ltd. pp 208-213.

Anastasi, A. (1997). *Psychological Testing*. Delhi : Pearson.

Avila, J.V. (1979). A Study of the Effects of Selected Teaching Competencies on Secondary Student Achievement. In *Dissertation Abstracts International* (1979), 39 (11), pp. 6493-6494-A.

Bajwa, S. (2003). Effectiveness of Competency-Based Teacher Training Strategy. *Journal of Indian Education*, New Delhi: NCERT, pp. 30-37.

Barbara and F Ield. (1994). The Skills and Competencies of Beginning Teachers. *In Barbara and Terry,* F. (Ed.), *Teachers as Mentors : A Practical Guide*. London: Falmer Press.

Barnes, L.R. and Taylor, C.S. (1988). Teacher Competency and the Primary School Curriculum : A Survey of Five Schools in North-East England. *British Educational Research Journal*, Vol. 14, No. 3. pp. 283.

Best, John W. and Kahn James V. (2008). *Research in Education*. New Delhi : Prentice-Hall of India Private Limited.

Birla Ambani Report. (1998). *A report submitted in Prime Minister's Office,* New Delhi.

Borich, G. D. and Fenton, K. S. (1977). *The Appraisal of Teaching Concepts and Process.* NY : Wesley Publishing Company.

Chaudhury, K. (1989). Teaching of Concepts Through the Concept Attainment Model and Facts Through Traditional Teaching : Competency in Teaching Skills of Pre-Service Teachers. In Buch, M.B. (Ed.), *Fifth Survey of Educational Research* (1988-92), Vol. II, New Delhi : NCERT, p. 1405.

Chaudhury, K. (1990). An Exploratory Study to find out the Impact of Teachers Personality on Competency in Advance Organizer Model and Inductive Thinking Model. *Journal of Educational Research and Extension,* 27 (1), New Delhi: NCERT. pp. 36-51.

Das, R. C., Jangira, N. K., Singh, A. and Passi, B. K. (1998). A Study of Effect of Intervention Training in the Integration of Teaching Competency of Student Teachers. In Buch, M.B. (Ed.), *Fifth Survey of Educational Research* (1988-92), Vol. II, New Delhi : NCERT, p. 1364.

Dave, C. S. (1987). A Study of Relative Effectiveness of Microteaching having Summative Model of Integration Versus Mini-Teaching Model in Terms of General Teaching Competence. In Buch, M.B. (Ed.), *Fourth Survey of Research in Education* (1991), Vol. II, New Delhi : NCERT, p. 931.

Delors, J. (1996). *Learning: The Treasure Within.* Bangkok : UNESCO.

Dictionary of Education (1981). Rowntree, D. London : Harper and Row Publishers.

Dictionary of Education (1997). S. K. Singh (Ed.), Vol.-1, Commonwealth Publisher.

Encyclopaedic Dictionary of Education (1997). Mehndiratta, M. New Delhi: Sarup and Sons.

Farah (2002). A Comparative Study of Teaching Competencies of the Teachers Trained through the Formal System of Education and those through the Distance Education

System. Unpublished Ph.D. thesis, *IASE, Faculty of Education,* Jamia Millia Islamia, New Delhi.

Garret, H. E. (1962). *Statistics in Psychology and Education.* Bombay : Allied Pacific.

Goel D. R., Goel Chhaya and Jasrani, Sucheta. (2000). Primary School Education Lost in Management. In *'Management of Primary Education – A Challenge'. Rao Pura,* Varoda : Good Comparian.

Good, Carter V. (2008). *Introduction to Educational Research: Methodology of Design in the Behavioural and Social Sciences.* Delhi : Surjeet Publications.

Guilford, J. P. (1984). *Psychometric Methods.* New Delhi : Tata-Mc- Graw Hill.

Hall, G. E. and Jones, H. L. (1976). *Competency Based Education : A Process for the Improvement of Education.* New Jerrey : Prentice-Hall.

Hall, P.H. (2001). Perceptions of Beginning Elementary Teachers and Elementary Principals Regarding the Preparedness of Beginning Teachers as Related to Stated Competencies. In *Dissertation Abstracts International* (2001), 62 (5), p. 1800-A.

International Dictionary of Education (1978). Page, G. T. and Thomas, J. B. NY : Nichole Publishing Company.

Jablonski, A.M. (1996). The influence of Pre-service Teachers' Cognition, Behaviour, And Perceived Self Efficacy on Teaching Performance during a mentored Internship. In *Dissertation Abstracts International* (1997), 57(10), p. 4332-A.

Joshi, S. M. and Kumar, S. (1983). Effect of the Skill-Based Approach and Decision-Making Ability on the Development of Teaching Competence. In Buch, M. B. (Ed.), *Fifth Survey of Educational Research* (1988-92), Vol.II, New Delhi : NCERT, p. 1410.

Kerlinger, Fred N. (2007). *Foundations of Behavioural Research.* Delhi : Surjeet Publications.

Khantachvana, P. (1994). Competencies for a Technical Education Curriculum: Perceptions of Technical Education,

Teachers in Bangkok, Thailand. In *Dissertation Abstracts International* (1995), 56 (3), p. 781-A.

Lalitha, M. S. (1981). Effectiveness of a Strategy of Training for Intergrating Teaching Skills on Teaching Competence of Student Teachers. In Buch, M.B. (Ed.). *Fourth Survey of Research in Education,* Vol.II, New Delhi : NCERT, pp. 956-957.

Leou, S. (1998). *Teaching Competencies Assessment Approaches for Mathematics Teachers.* Proc. Natt. Sci. Counc. ROC (D), Vol. 8, (3), pp. 102-107.

Maddox, A. L. (1994). Teacher Competencies needed by new Secondary Vocational Instructors in Georgia. In *Dissertation Abstracts International*. (1995), 56 (3), p. 903-A.

Mutawa, A. (2002). *Evaluation of EFL Primary School Teachers' Competencies in Kuwait.* Curriculum and Instruction Department, Faculty of Education, Kuwait University, Kuwait.

Naseema, C. (1994). A Study of Teaching Competence of Secondary School Physical Science Teachers in Relation to Satisfaction of Teaching Physical Science. *In Indian Educational Abstracts* (1996), pp. 1, 42.

NCTE (1998). *Competency Based and Commitment Oriented Teacher Education for Quality School Education*. New Delhi : National Council for Teacher Education.

Nelson, B.C. (1988). A Study of Relationship between Teacher Competency and Pupil Achievement. In *Dissertation Abstracts International* (1989), 49(8), p. 2055-A.

Panchalan, R. (2004). Competency Development and Training. New Delhi: *Employment News*. (28 February - 5 March).

Pandey, K. P. (2005). *Fundamentals of Educational Research.* Varanasi: Vishwavidyalaya Prakashan.

Pandya, M. J. (1991). A Study of the Relative Effectiveness of Micro-Teaching and the Traditional Technique of Teacher Training in the Development of General Teaching Competence of the Student Teachers of Secondary Teachers Training College. In Buch, M.B. (Ed.). *Fifth*

Survey of Educational Research (1988-92), Vol. II, New Delhi : NCERT, p. 1384.

Passi, B. K. and Lalitha, M. S. (1994). *Manual for General Teaching Competency Scale (GTCS).* Agra : National Psychological Corporation.

Prakasham, D. (1986). A Study of Teacher Effectiveness as a Function of School Organizational Climate and Teaching Competency. In M.B. Buch (Ed.), *Fourth Survey of Research in Education* (1991), Vol.II, New Delhi : NCERT, p. 1036.

Prakasham, D. (1988). A Study of Teacher Effectiveness as a Function of School Organisational Climate and Teaching Competency. In Buch, M. B. (Ed.), *Fourth Survey of Research in Education* (1991), Vol. II, New Delhi : NCERT, pp. 1465-1466.

Probe Report. (1998). *World Bank Report.* Peris.

Raju, B. and Viswanathappa A. (2007). Competency of D.Ed. and B.Ed. trained Teachers working in Primary Schools of Andhra Pradesh. EDUTRACKS, Sept. 2007, Vol. 7, (1), Hyderabad : Neelkamal Publications Pvt. Ltd., pp. 29-33.

Rama, M. (1979). Factorial Structure of Teaching Competencies among Secondary School Teachers. Unpublished Doctoral Dissertation, M. S. University of Baroda, Baroda.

Rao, D. B. (1998). *District Primary Education Programme.* New Delhi : Discovery Publishing House.

Rao, D. B. (Ed.). (1998). *Teacher Education in India.* New Delhi: Discovery Publishing House.

Saeed, M. and Mahmood, K. (2002). Assessing Competency of Pakistani Primary School Teachers in Mathematics, Science and Pedagogy. *International Journal of Educational Management,* MCB UP Ltd. Vol.:16, (4), pp. 190-195.

Shanbhag, S.P. (2007). *Effectiveness of a Mastery Learning Instructional Strategy in Attainment of Competencies in Mathematics.* From http://www.aiaer.net/ejournal.

Sharma, M. L. (1979). A Study into the Development of Teacher Competencies of the B.Ed. Student Teachers in the Training Colleges of Rajasthan. In Buch, M. B. (Ed.), *Third Survey of Research in Education* (1986), New Delhi : NCERT, pp. 840-841.

Sharma, R. A. (2000). *Essentials of Scientific Behavioural Research.* Meerut : Surya.

Singh, A. K. (2002). *Tests, Measurements and Research Methods in Behavioural Sciences.* Patna : Bharati Bhawan.

Singh, L.C. (1989). A Study of Relative Effectiveness of Two Training Strategies in Developing Teaching Competency and Attitude towards Teaching among Student-Teachers. In Buch, M.B. (Ed.), *Fifth Survey of Educational Research* (2000), Vol. II, New Delhi : NCERT, pp. 1390-1391.

Singh, S. (2004). A Study of Factors Influencing Teaching Competency of Primary School Teachers. *Unpublished Ph. D. Thesis*, Department of Education, University of Lucknow, Lucknow.

Singh, Seema (2008). A Study of Teaching Competency of Secondary School Teachers in Relation to Gender and Teaching Experience. *Indian Journal of Educational Research,* July-December 2008, Vol. 27, No. 2, Lucknow : Bhartiya Shiksha Sodh Sansthan. pp. 63-68.

Singh, V. (2004). A Study of the Effect of B.Ed. Training Programme on Teaching Competency of Pupil Teachers. *Unpublished Ph. D. Thesis*, Department of Education, University of Lucknow, Lucknow.

Smart, R. (2003). A Study of Professional Commitment of Primary School Teachers in Relation to Working Condition and Selected personal Factors. *Unpublished Ph. D. Thesis,* Department of Education, University of Lucknow, Lucknow.

Springer, P.L. (2000). How Pre-Service Teachers Incorporate Technology Into Lessons During Their Practice Teaching Experience : An Intrinsic Case Study. In *Dissertation Abstracts International* (2001), 61(7), p. 2673-A.

Srinivasan, V. (1992). Personality Traits of Primary School Teachers and their Attitude towards Teaching. *Fifth Survey of Educational Research*, (1988-92), Vol. II, New Delhi : NCERT, p. 1491.

Thamilmani, P. (1990). A Study of Teacher Competency and Teacher Personality in relation to Achievement of High

School Students in Science. In Buch, M.B. (Ed.), *Fifth Survey of Educational Research* (2000), 2, New Delhi : NCERT, p. 1926.

The International Encyclopaedia of Education (1985). Husen, T. and Postlethwaite, T. N. (Ed.). Oxford : Pergamon Press Limited.

Tuckman, B. W. *Measuring Educational Outcomes : Fundamental of Teaching.* New York : Harcourt Brace Jovanovic Inc.

Vashishtha, U. C. (2001). A Project entitled *'A Feedback Study of DPEP Input in Teachers Training Programme of U. P.'* Allahabad : SIEMAT.

Vashishtha, U. C., Shukla, Anil and Trivedi, T. (2001). *Private School Allure : An Introspection.* Published in 'Perspectives in Education'. Vadodara : CASE, pp. 114-116.

Verma, B. S. (1998). A Study of Developing Teaching Competency among Student-Teachers of Science Group through Micro-Teaching. In Buch, M.B. (Ed.), *Fifth Survey of Educational Research* (2000), Vol. II, New Delhi : NCERT, p. 1398.

Viswanathappa G. (2005). Attitude towards Teaching and Teaching Competence. *EDUTRACKS*, August, 2005, Vol. 4, (12), Hyderabad, Neelkamal Publications Pvt. Ltd., pp. 21-27.

Walker (1992). *Teachers as Mentors: A Practical Guide.* In Barbana and Terry, F. (Ed.), London : Falmer Press.

Warren, J. G. (1985). A Study of Relationship between Teacher Competencies and Student Cognitive Gain in Achievement on Criterion-Referenced Mathematics Tests : A Validation of a Teacher Assessment Instrument. *In Dissertation Abstracts International* (1986), 46 (8), p. 2161-A.

Watson, B. M. (1979). A Study of the Relationship of Age, Experience, Degrees, Prior Positions and School Size to Competencies in Seven Selected Job Functions as Perceived by Principals of Indian Public Secondary Schools. In *Dissertation Abstracts International* (1980), 40 (8), p. 4345-A.

Webster's Third New International Dictionary on-the English Language. (1964). Philip, B. G. (Ed.). London: G Bell and Sons Limited.

Index

A

Acharya Ramamurti Committee Report (1992), 45

Administration, 94, 49

And Scoring Procedure, 90

Advance Organizer Model, (AOM), 65

American Psychological Association, 94

Art

Group, 142, 146

Stream, 146

Stream Teachers, 150, 155

Assessment, 37

Assessment Guide and Micro-Teaching Lesson-Plan, 69

Audio-Visual Aids, 54

B

Birla Ambani Report, 51

C

CAT

Post-Test Scores, 62

Pre-Test Scores, 62

Child

Development, 44, 45

Psychology, 54

Classroom

Management, 37, 54

Observation Techniques, 68

Colonial Period, 49

Communication Revolution, 28

Community Support for Schools, 49

Competencies, 29-37

Based Curriculum, 48

Based Evaluation System, 48

Class Related, 40

Community Related, 40

Competency Based Education, 31

Competency Based Teacher Education, 32

Competency Based Teaching, 31

Consequence, 34

Content, 44

Contextual, 42-43

Curriculum Related, 41

Defined, 29, 31, 32

Development, 30

Evaluation, 48

Generic, 36
Knowledge, 34
Pupil Related, 40
School Related, 40
Teaching, 30
Transactional, 45
Value Related, 41
Competency
Based Teaching of Environmental Sciences, 73
Comprehensive List of-, 38
In Teaching Special Students, 70
Measuring Tools, 86
Cultural Events, 46

D

Dave Committee Report, 44
Delphi Method, 68
Descriptive Survey Methods, 80
Detors' Report, 51
Development of Teachers Competencies, 58
Directive Principles of State Policy, 26
Distance Learners, 74
District
Lakhimpur Khasi, 51
Lucknow, 53, 55, 81, 151
Primary Education Program (DPEP), 27
Raipur and Bilaspur, 63
Dropout Rate of Primary Level, 50

E

Early Childhood Teachers, 36
Education, 25
Commission (1964-1966), 50
Compulsory, 26
Elementary, 48
For All, 51
For Development, 26
Higher, 25
In India, 26
Of Teachers, 27
Primary, 27
Primary and Elementary, 28
School, 25, 26, 28
Secondary, 25
Universalization of
Elementary Education, 25, 48
Primary-(UPE), 26, 27, 28
Primary- in India, 27
Educational
Changes, 26
Implications, 44
Election, 37
Empowerment, 25
Environmental Sciences, 73

F

Female Teachers, 64, 100, 151

Field Survey Techniques, 59

Five Major Teaching Competencies, (FMTC), 97, 102, 114, 115, 141

- Content Competencies, 97, 102, 110, 114, 115, 121, 128, 136, 141, 147, 150-154
- Contextual Competencies, 106, 118, 119, 128, 132, 151, 152
- Development of Teaching Learning Material, 97, 102, 112, 114, 115, 129, 139, 141, 150, 151, 153
- Educational Activities Competency, 97, 102, 103, 104, 108, 114, 116, 118, 127—
- Transactional Competencies, 97, 102, 108, 114, 115, 120, 127, 134, 141, 145, 151, 152, 153, 155

Formal System of Education, 71

G

GRCS (General Teaching Competency Scale), 63

Group Learning, 28

H

Higher Education Institutions, 36, 44

Human Rights, 27

I

Indore Teaching Competencies School, 59

Inductive Thinking Model (ITM), 65

Industrial Area Schools, 61

Initial Teacher Education Program, 36

Instructional

- Competencies Technology, 70
- Training Laboratory (ITC), 68

Inter-Agency Commission, 50

Inter-Related Categories of Competencies, 42

K

Knowledge Competencies, 33

L

Leadership Role Model, 41

Learning

- Resources, 47
- Teaching Practices, (LTP), 49, 55

Level of

- Teaching Competency (ies), 98, 151

Literacy, 27

M

Madurai Kamraj University, 74

Major Reforms, 28
  School Curriculum, 28
  Textbook-cum-Workbook, 28
Management
  Competencies, 48
  Of Multi-grade Classroom, 47
Mathematics Teachers, 68
Micro-Teaching
  Scale, 65
  Skills, 69
  Vs Mini Teaching Model, 61
Minimum Levels of Learning (MLL), 28

N

National
  Council of Measuring, 94
  Events, 46
  Policy on Education (NPE), 28, 45
New Teachers Institutions, (NTIs), 67
Non-Formal Education System, 28

O

ONGC Centre, 47
Open School Organization Climate, 63, 64
Operation Black Board (OB), 28

P

Physical Science Teachers, 67
Planning, 36, 57, 87
Planning Procedure, 79
Practice Teaching, 45
Pre-Service
  Professional Training, 123, 124
  Teachers, 70
  Primary Education, 50, 51, 52
  School Children Enrolment of-, 51
  School Teachers (PST), 37-39, 50, 51-55, 90, 151, 72, 73, 95
    Competencies, 54
    Competencies in Kuwait, 70
    Dimensions of-, 90
    Of Lucknow District, 81, 83, 97
    Personality Traits, 66
    Teaching Competencies, 81, 83, 86, 97-150, 151-159
  Schools, 51, 62
Private Unaided Schools, 73
Professional
  Development, 69
  Training, 116, 122, 153, 156
Professionalism, 37
Public Secondary Schools, 59

Q

Quality of Education for All, 25

R

Research
- Designs, 79
- Methodology, 79
- Problems, 97

Role of Community, 49

S

SCERT Lucknow, 83

SCERT Report (UP), 51

School
- Accountability, 33
- Organization Climate, 63, 64

Schooling Facilities, 50

Schools Types, 52
- Parishadiya, 52
- Private, 52

Schools under Christian Management, 64

Science
- Stream, 155
- Teachers, 66

Science and
- Art Stream, 150
- Commerce Stream, 153, 155

Scientific and Technological Development Impacts, 43

Self-Learning, 28

Senior Secondary Teachers, 36

Social
- And Cultural System, 43
- And National Development, 25
- Scientists Activities, 37

Societies, Progressive, 25

Society, 25, 28

Socio-Economic
- Advancement, 25
- Background of Students, 61, 62
- Status, 58

Special Orientation Program for Teachers, (SOPT), 28

Staff Development Program, 58

T

Teacher
- Attitude Inventory, 69
- Behaviour
  - Characteristics, 58
- Competencies, 40, 62, 65, 66, 67, 74, 75, 81, 151, 153, 154, 155, 156, 157
- Competencies Types, 33
- Directed Learning, 28, 46
- Education, 25, 26, 28
- Education Process,
- Education Program, 45
- Effectiveness, 63, 64
  - Scale, 63
  - Job, 43

Performance Observation Record, 60
Personality, 65
Philosophy and Guidance, 33

Teachers
Training Colleges, 58, 62
Transfer of-, 27

Teaching
Learning Aids, 28
Learning Material, (TLM), 46, 123-125, 128-130, 139, 140, 148, 153-155
Learning Process in India, 45
Methods and Competencies, 70
Practices, 68
Process, 30

Teaching
Competency (ies), (TC), 30, 54, 57, 58, 61, 64, 65, 66, 68, 69, 74, 86, 87, 90, 97, 98, 100-102, 106, 108, 110, 114-116, 118, 122, 124-126, 128-130, 134, 136, 141, 142, 143, 148
Major Teaching Competencies, 87
Scale, 59
Scores, 60, 71
Test, 86, 116, 128, 129, 139, 141, 150, 155

Technical Teachers of Bangkok (Thailand), 67

Technological Advancement, 28

Technology and Assessment, 69

Trained Teachers, 156

Training
Colleges of Rajasthan, 58
Programs, 30, 156

Types of Competencies for Primary School Teachers, (TCPST), 50
Competencies to Develop Teaching Learning Materials, 50
Content Competencies, 50
Contextual, 50
Related to Evaluation Activities, 50
Transactional, 50

Types of Researches, 80
Descriptive, 80
Experimental, 80
Historical, 80

U

Unemployment, 43

Universalization, 25
Of Elementary Education, 48

Urbanization, 43

V

Value Inculcation, 43

W

World
Conference on Education for All (WCEFA), 50
Trade Organization (WTO) Agreement, 51